The Overseas Chinese of South East Asia

Also by Ian Rae and Morgen Witzel

SINGULAR AND DIFFERENT: BUSINESS IN CHINA PAST PRESENT AND FUTURE

Also by Morgen Witzel

BIOGRAPHICAL DICTIONARY OF MANAGEMENT
BUILDERS AND DREAMERS: THE MAKING AND MEANING OF MANAGEMENT
ENCYCLOPEDIA OF THE HISTORY OF AMERICAN MANAGEMENT
HOW TO GET AN MBA
FIFTY KEY FIGURES IN MANAGEMENT
MANAGEMENT: THE BASICS
DOING BUSINESS IN CHINA *(with Tim Ambler)*
JOHN ADAIR *(with Jonathan Gosling and Peter Case)*
MANAGING IN VIRTUAL ORGANIZATIONS *(with Malcolm Warner)*

The Overseas Chinese of South East Asia

History, Culture, Business

Ian Rae and Morgen Witzel

palgrave
macmillan

Softcover reprint of the hardcover 1st edition 2008 978-1-4039-9165-2

First published 2008 by
PALGRAVE MACMILLAN
Houndmills, Basingstoke, Hampshire RG21 6XS and
175 Fifth Avenue, New York, N.Y. 10010
Companies and representatives throughout the world

PALGRAVE MACMILLAN is the global academic imprint of the Palgrave Macmillan division of St. Martin's Press, LLC and of Palgrave Macmillan Ltd. Macmillan® is a registered trademark in the United States, United Kingdom and other countries. Palgrave is a registered trademark in the European Union and other countries.

ISBN 978-1-349-54304-5 ISBN 978-0-230-59312-1 (eBook)

DOI 10.1057/9780230593121

This book is printed on paper suitable for recycling and made from fully managed and sustained forest sources. Logging, pulping and manufacturing processes are expected to conform to the environmental regulations of the country of origin.

A catalogue record for this book is available from the British Library.

A catalogue record for this book is available from the Library of Congress.

10 9 8 7 6 5 4 3 2 1
17 16 15 14 13 12 11 10 09 08

Transferred to Digital Printing 2011

Contents

Preface

In our previous work on China, *Singular and Different*, we devoted a single chapter to the Overseas Chinese. This book now looks at the subject in more detail: where the Chinese came from and why they settled in the region, how they got there and how they fared. We describe how they came to dominate the economy of South-East Asia, the difficulties they have overcome, and their contribution not only to business but also to society and politics. This includes the various wars and revolutions that occurred in the region during World War II and thereafter. We also recount how the stupendous growth of modern China depends greatly on these compatriots from overseas. As we have quoted before, 'within the four seas, all men are brothers'.

Ian Rae
Morgen Witzel

1
Introduction

The Chinese first settled in South-East Asia or Nanyang over 2,000 years ago, establishing small trading posts, which in time grew and prospered. There was little contact with local inhabitants and their presence was tolerated by the regional rulers. Later, unrest and periodic upheaval in China encouraged further emigration, which reached significant proportions in the 19th century. By this time the region, with the exception of Thailand, had been colonised by Western powers and the resultant economic expansion gave further impetus to the influx of Chinese labour. Meanwhile Chinese settlers, by dint of enterprise, hard work and concerted effort had come to control much of the economy. Japanese occupation during World War II dislodged the colonial powers, who after a short lived return granted independence throughout the region. The countries of South-East Asia are today mostly stable and prosperous; their Chinese minorities are now largely assimilated politically and their economic strength is accepted. They also play a leading role in the advance of modern China; the Overseas Chinese now providing a large part of all the foreign investment. Relations between the Peoples Republic of China and the Chinese of South-East Asia are excellent and close ties are encouraged. The Chinese from China differ in many ways from the Chinese from the rest of the region although they still have much in common. All look to China as their ancestral home and all share a consciousness of what has been aptly called 'Chineseness'. This encompasses certain traditional ethics and values: the acceptance of a hierarchical society, the importance of family and community, the attendant ties and loyalties, the value of learning. They also share a difficult and complex language with some of the spoken Chinese dialects mutually unintelligible. Yet all Chinese write the same, wherever they may be.

For a long time the inhabitants of the countries in which the Chinese settled, be they adjoining China with a common, or near common, land frontier or much further away and separated by sea, looked askance in varying degree at these new arrivals. In some cases, where there was already a slight degree of cultural and linguistic affinity there was in time a measure of assimilation; in those where there was no such link, none at all. There was often dislike and suspicion of the newcomers, with their clannish ways, cohesive social structure and refusal to abandon or even modify any cultural differences. Over the years this hostility began to abate and, depending on the territory, varying degrees of mutual collaboration ensued. In the main, the Chinese left any politics to the locals and a tacit acceptance of this divide spread through much of the region. But it was by no means plain sailing and there was often friction. What in time transformed the situation was the enterprise, business acumen and mutual cooperation between themselves – of the Overseas Chinese or Huaqiao, their name in Chinese, who control most of the business life of Nanyang, though they consist of but a fraction of the total population.

Hua is the Mandarin pronunciation of the Chinese character meaning flowery, which also stands for China, *qiao* for the character meaning to live abroad, thus Huaqiao, sojourners abroad i.e. Overseas Chinese. Nan means south, yang means ocean, Nanyang, the southern ocean, i.e. South-East Asia. The countries in which they settled fall into two main categories: those that abut China and were for many years within the orbit of some Chinese cultural influence, albeit remotely, and had some tenuous connection such as their rulers sending annual tribute to the Emperor, and the rest further away and harder to reach, where in the old days China had no influence of any form what so ever. Later on both these categories were greatly influenced by a major influx of the Chinese that changed them forever. There are many accounts of these Chinese who settled, what they were like, how they fared, how they suffered, how they succeeded, together with descriptions of the host countries and their mutual relationships. The main impact of all this was on the various regional economies, but politics came to play a role too on occasion. There have been wars, rebellions, risings and riots, some completely self-contained, some subject to outside influence, some post-war struggles for independence from Western rule.

The Chinese settlers who mainly came from the southeastern seaboard of China spoke varying dialects, and only a small minority were literate in their complex written language. Over time, some came to learn the totally different languages of their countries of adoption, often in a bastardised form, enough for simple contact, no more. There was little social or intellectual exchange, save on the part of a few; most were too busy trying to make a living. There was an earlier cultural affinity with China that existed, and still exists in part, in the states closer to China. Vietnamese, Burmese, Thai, Lao are tonal language, as is Chinese, though the written script is totally different. There is a little common vocabulary. The chief religion in all these countries, and China, was and remains Buddhism; there is some Taoism and small minorities are Muslims and Christians. Travel south, and a curtain of cultural incomprehension descends. The Malay language or Bahasa Malaysia, Bahasa Indonesia, Javanese, Batak, Sunda, Sulawesi, Filipino, Tagalog, Visayan, Moro, etc. are all atonal languages with a structure and syntax totally removed from Chinese. Some were originally written in Sanskrit, then later in Arabic script, a legacy of the Arab traders who first began to bring Islam to the region from the late 7th century onwards; all are now romanised. With the exception of the Roman Catholic Philippines, and some Protestants in Molucca, nearly all the people are Muslims. The only exception to these generalities is Singapore which has been almost entirely Chinese for 200 years.

China is now stronger and richer than ever before, her people more prosperous, albeit with great pockets of poverty, industry booming, modernising fast, and a huge balance of trade surplus. The government presides over a mostly orderly transition from a form of communism to a form of capitalism. It was only just over half a century ago that Mao Zedong proclaimed the People's Republic on 1st October 1949, assuming the rule of a country devastated by close on a generation of war. Liberation, as it was called, followed a quarter of a century of civil war, a brutal and savage all out attack by Japan in 1937 until Allied victory in World War II, then finally more civil war. Before that, in the late 19th century, a weak and crumbling empire had largely lost its economic independence to an acquisitive and aggressive West that controlled banking, foreign trade and most of what little industry there was. The new People's government went to work with a will; imposed a command economy, entered a period of reconstruction and attempted the transformation of society. All went well until a series of catastrophic blunders, chiefly the Great Leap Forward which aimed to speedily increase production, followed not long after by the Cultural Revolution which aimed to remould society but was in reality a bid to reassert total power by Mao, undid much of the progress made. Throughout this time there was great suffering and millions died.

Things really began to change in 1978 with the Open Door policy which, among others, welcomed foreign investment and over time introduced a controlled private enterprise system to co-exist with the command economy; growth has accelerated ever since. China is no longer a sealed country; Chinese travel abroad by the thousands, likewise Westerners travel over most of China. Earlier announced aims of liberating, that is communising, have long since been abandoned for a pragmatic approach and close relations with her Asian neighbours; the hostility and suspicion of 40 or 50 years ago has gone, though traces remain. Relations with the rest of the world, with one or two exceptions, are good. China's economy grows at 9% a year and there is little sign yet of it slowing down.

This background of dramatic change in China has of course impinged upon the well-established economy of Nanyang. This includes the various types and categories of commercial enterprises: the long established, powerful and successful Chinese-founded trading houses and banks, the myriads of small businesses, the Western businesses that have adapted and remain, the far fewer and mostly recently established similar organisations run by the indigenous people, some with government support. There are now more industries, long-established ones such as textiles, electrics, plastics, shipbuilding; the newer high technology: also extractives such as tin, bauxite, wolfram mining industries, oil exploration and drilling etc. Agriculture still plays a very big part, much of it modernised and up to a point mechanised: rubber, tea, coffee, tobacco, palm oil, and logging. Small plantations continue and some peasants still plough their rice fields with wooden ploughs drawn by water buffaloes. Most trading activities are largely but not entirely Overseas Chinese-owned and operated, including much of industry. Recently there have emerged more partnerships between local people and the Chinese, each realising what the other can offer. Some of the regional governments further intervene to varying degrees, particularly in encouraging cross-cultural activity and investment. This is again generally supported by Huaqiao as well as the indigenous people. The nations of South-East Asia which belong to the various global organizations that sponsor trade, industry and banking are increasingly playing their part.

From the 19th and early 20th century onwards, Europeans dominated the commercial scene in Nanyang principally because they had the backing of their respective colonial governments; indeed there was often little to choose between the government official and plantation manager. Young men came out from Europe to join the big trading houses or become managers on the new rubber estates. No training or qualifications were necessary, just the right connections and background. In time, many of these European firms worked alongside the local Chinese merchants who knew the market and local conditions far better, not unlike the compradores on the China coast, a system whereby a Chinese merchant bought and sold for foreigners at his discretion and on his account. Meanwhile the aristocracy of the various South-East Asian races mostly eschewed commerce, though a few princelings were occasionally offered positions and fat retainers, purely to buy their influence. When World War II smashed the old systems, and also nearly ruined the regional economy it seemed these earlier arrangement were gone forever. But it only took a couple of years after victory in 1945 for much of the old to return. However this was short-lived; European supremacy was very soon over as these countries became independent and were politicised. The Westerners who stayed on did so on different terms. These societies have been transformed and with marked exception are now wealthier, better educated and more egalitarian.

There are also two different yet in some ways similar territories: Singapore and Hong Kong; both are Chinese, free of any racial or ethnic tensions, high-tech, small, economically successful, efficient, with excellent business and banking. Here of course the similarities end. Hong Kong is not part of South-East Asia, however it is included as it impinges so closely. Its people are almost all Cantonese, as are many Overseas Chinese, and thus originate from the same part of China. From the latter half of the 19th century onwards, a good proportion of the European and Chinese traders and businessmen in South-East Asia had back-up, or connections with Hong Kong which since then, has more recently become the engine that drives much of the development of South China. Much of the investment that now flows into China comes through Hong Kong, of that, a good part is from South-East Asia. Singapore is a Chinese city state, most of its population Hokkien, also originally from the seaboard of Southeast China. A few of its inhabitants are descended from families settled hundreds of years ago, the so-called Straits born; most are more recent arrivals in the late 19th and early 20th century; all have made the island state the commercial and banking hub of South-East Asia. Its highly skilled workforce is at the forefront of technology, its businessmen and bankers run successful enterprises focused both regionally and internationally. When business interests in Indonesia, or the Philippines, or elsewhere in Nanyang want a safe haven for their money they look to Singapore or Hong Kong and for capital they do likewise.

These different countries and disparate societies make up Nanyang. Throughout, Chinese have settled to exert an economic influence far in excess of their numbers, now increasingly in partnership with the indigenous population. They have also come to play a significant role in society and politics and are accepted throughout the region; the previous resentment and discrimination has very largely disappeared. The Huaqiao are responsible for much of the massive investment that now flows into China. However, with the growing economic power of China itself, their relative importance has begun to decline.

Not for the first time, the Overseas Chinese face a future which is not entirely clear. Old certainties are disappearing, and the old order in South-East Asia is changing. Politically and economically, the region as whole is going forward; but not every country is moving at the same speed, and a few states such as Burma and Laos are lagging behind. It seems certain that South-East Asia's role in the world economy will change considerably over the next two decades. This change will present problems for Western and local businesses alike. And, because of their continuing economic power, the Huaqiao will almost certainly be at the centre of any change.

This book sets out to describe the Overseas Chinese on several levels. It looks at the people themselves, their culture and history, their identity as migrants, exiles or refugees settling in foreign lands, and the receptions they received from the indigenous populations, ranging from friendly to hostile. It looks at South-East Asia's long historical role as a trading partner both with China and with India and Western Europe, and the role played by the Chinese community in facilitating that trade. Historically a producer of luxury goods such as spices or raw materials such as oil, rubber and copra in the late 20th century, the region developed rapidly into a manufacturing centre. We look too at the growing and changing business cultures of the region and how these cultures affect Western businesses operating in the region.

In Chapter 2, we set the scene and look at the origins of the Overseas Chinese community. We describe how the first Chinese migrants began arriving in South-East Asia, and the extensive growth of that community in the 19th century. Many of these early migrants were indentured labourers, but as time went by they established businesses and became part of the middle classes of their host countries. Inevitably this created tensions, and relations between the Huaqiao and the indigenous population were not always smooth. World War II created much hardship for both populations. Then came the establishment of the People's Republic of China, which exacerbated tensions; Overseas

Chinese were often accused of sympathy with the communist government in Beijing, and of fomenting rebellion in the host countries. Sometimes these accusations were false, sometimes they were true; in Malaysia and Indonesia, there were communist elements among the Overseas Chinese, and in Malaysia in particular these participated in a bloody war against the British colonial government. Since then, however, tensions have eased, and despite occasional flare-ups, by and large the two groups live in peace.

In Chapter 3, we begin a more detailed examination, looking first at those countries of the northern mainland of South-East Asia: Burma, Thailand, Vietnam, Cambodia and Laos. These countries, being geographically closest to China, have also been the most subject to Chinese influence. In the past, when the Chinese empire was strong, China aspired to rule this region and sometimes extracted tribute from local governments, in Vietnam especially. Among these five countries, there is however a great deal of diversity. Burma, under the oppressive rule of SLORC, remains poor, backward and isolated, probably more so than any other country in the region. Ongoing rebellions by ethnic groups in the north and east have led to a state of low-level civil war in parts of the country. Laos, taken over by the communist government of the Pathet Lao in the 1960s, remains strongly influenced by Vietnam, and also remains poor and backward, most of its people engaged in agriculture. Cambodia, embroiled in the Vietnam conflict, then endured the three years of horror of Khmer Rouge rule, and even 30 years on is still scarred by that conflict. Vietnam, on the other hand, is making strides towards development, and is beginning to emerge from the shadows. The last country in the region is Thailand, the great enigma of South-East Asia. Unlike every other country in the region, it was never colonised by Europe, although its government was heavily dominated by French interests. Thailand has always pursued a slightly different path from its neighbours; today, it is the strongest and most prosperous country among the five we discuss, and not by coincidence, it is also the country that has traditionally been most welcoming to Chinese immigrants.

Chapter 4 turns south and east to countries more distant from China and therefore less directly influenced by it. These include Malaysia, part of mainland South-East Asia, but ethnically strongly related to the island states beyond, and then Singapore, the great sprawling archipelago of Indonesia and, further north, the Philippines. These four states are very distinct from the five nations we looked at previously. Islam, not Buddhism, is the dominant religion; although the majority of the population of the Philippines is Catholic, there is a strong minority Muslim population. Culturally and linguistically they are different too, with languages like Malay and Tagalog being quite distinct from the Chinese family of languages spoken further north. Yet here again, there are exceptions. Singapore is the most obvious one, a largely ethnic Chinese enclave created under British colonial rule and with strong cultural ties to China. Malaysia has a large Chinese population which plays a major role in the economy; Indonesia has proportionally a very small Chinese population, but these are if anything even more prominent in the economy. Indonesia and the Philippines are also very ethnically diverse countries, despite the attempts at 'Javanisation' by the authorities in Jakarta in the years after independence.

Chapter 5 looks back at the ancestral country, China, and how the changes in China have in turn meant changes for the Overseas Chinese. One of the abiding characteristics of the Huaqiao is their tendency to maintain strong links with their homeland. The ties of family are very strong in Chinese culture, and are not easily broken. In the 1920s and 1930s those ties became critically important to China, as support from the overseas community allowed the Nationalist government of Chiang Kai-Shek to hold back the communists and the invading Japanese. With the beginnings of economic reform in China in the late 1970s, those ties again became important; as noted above, the Huaqiao provided a significant proportion of the investment that helped China to develop into a world economic superpower in fewer than 30 years. Now, as China becomes increasingly strong, the balance of power is changing and the relationship between the Huaqiao and China is changing too.

In Chapter 6, we look at language and culture. The Huaqiao often come from many different ethnic backgrounds in China, and originally many had no common spoken language, though of course all who were literate could read written Chinese. Today, both English and Mandarin are widely spoken, both serving as lingua francas for business negotiations. Most Overseas Chinese also learn the language of their host nation: Thai, Malay, Tagalog, Vietnamese, etc. A polyglot people, the Overseas Chinese also tend to be better educated than the indigenous population. Again, though, there are strong local variances depending on the country and the local culture, and Western visitors and business people need to be aware that there is no uniformity among the Overseas Chinese. There are common features, but there are also great differences.

In Chapter 7, we turn specifically to the economy of the region. South-East Asia has been a strong economic force for centuries. Even in the ancient world, South-East Asian products such as spices, incense, drugs and dyes travelled north to China but also west across the Indian Ocean, and then further west still to the Middle East and ultimately to Western Europe. By Roman times the spice trade had become economically important and valuable. As time passed, Chinese trade tended to wax and wane, and by the 15th century was in slow decline. By this time, though, the rising wealth and populations of both the Arab world and Western Europe had created large new markets. Arab traders arrived in the region first, bringing trade and also peacefully converting much of the population to Islam. Then came the Europeans. The Portuguese were first, establishing trading posts through a combination of diplomacy and force; the Spanish came soon after, but never expanded beyond the Philippines. When the ramshackle Portuguese empire collapsed the Dutch replaced them, settling down to rule the Indonesian archipelago and spreading their influence throughout the region. When Europe industrialised in the 19th century, the demand for other local products such as oil, rubber, teak, copra, tin and jute led to a new round of colonisation. By the end of the 19th century, only Thailand remained independent. Briefly, from 1941–1945, the European and American colonial masters were replaced by Imperial Japan, which exploited the region even more ruthlessly. The postwar period of independence saw a slow economic rebuilding. Throughout all this period, the Overseas Chinese had played an important economic role as middlemen, helping to facilitate trade. This helped them become prosperous, but also caused difficulties. Some local people saw the Chinese as complicit in colonial rule.

In Chapter 8, we look at the Asian 'miracle' that occurred in the years after the end of the Vietnam war. For all the damage the war inflicted, there were a few benefits, and one of these was the pump-priming effect that American military aid had on the Thai economy. Coincident with Thailand's steady growth came the arrival of Japanese investment. Japanese manufactures were looking for places to outsource production in order to keep costs down, and other Japanese businesses saw new market opportunities among the newly affluent Chinese-Thai middle classes. Investment led to economic growth which led to more investment. Malaysia spotted the opportunities too, and its 'Look East' policy also began attracting investment. Singapore began positioning itself as the region's economic capital. Gradually, Indonesia and the Philippines and even Vietnam began to join in. For a time, Thailand in particular enjoyed spectacular growth, as Western investment flooded in to replace Japanese capital in the 1990s. Then it all fell apart. The financial crisis that began in Thailand in 1997 quickly spread to the other countries of the region. Currencies collapsed, stock markets crashed, the IMF had to step in and put together rescue packages. Most importantly, though, while the South-East Asian economies wobbled, China remained secure. Chinese financial and economic stability, created in part by investment by the Huaqiao community, now helped save the South-East Asian economies.

In Chapter 9, we turn to examine the business cultures of South-East Asia. The dominant business model of the region remains, as it has for centuries, the so-called 'Chinese family business'. Even very large multinationals remain family-owned and controlled; more, they are structured and managed as if they were a family. Confucian values, with their emphasis on hierarchy, tradition and respect for elders, strongly influence the business culture of the Overseas Chinese community. There is also a strong emphasis on relationships; people prefer to do business with those they know and trust. Informal contacts are very important in building up such trust. Correspondingly, there is less of an emphasis on legal documents and formal negotiations, a fact which makes some American companies in particular feel rather nervous. However, the Chinese family model is not the only model. There are indigenous business models too, and over the course of time these have tended to influence each other. The way business is done in Thailand is different from the way business is done in Singapore; the differences are subtle, but they are there. Chapter 9 closes with a discussion of some of these differences. In Chapter 10, we then move on to the implications for Western businesses. How do Western businesses operate in this unfamiliar environment? How do they find markets? How do they build relationships with local businesses? Managing across cultures is a difficult and risky affair. What can Western managers do to lay off some of these risks?

Finally, in Chapter 11, we look at the future for South-East Asia, and for its Chinese community in particular. As we have noted, the old order is changing. China is now the dominant economic power in the region – and knows it. Beijing is increasingly making its voice heard and its presence felt. Overseas Chinese investment is still welcome in China, but is no longer the driving force behind the Chinese economy. South-East Asian manufacturers are finding it harder and harder to export to China as domestic production increases. Meanwhile, as the military coup d'etat in Thailand in 2006 showed, South-East Asia itself is still not politically, or economically, entirely stable. A new order is needed, and here Singapore, which has for some time been in the economic vanguard in South-East Asia, may be showing the way. The Huaqiao of South-East Asia have capital; they also have good educations and a large talent pool from which to draw. Singapore is increasingly turning to creative industries such as arts and film. Other countries of the region may see similar opportunities. In the 21st century, it may be that South-East Asia's greatest export opportunity lies not in pepper or nutmeg, rubber or tin or manufactured goods, but in the brains and talent of its people.

2
Nanyang and the Huaqiao

Nanyang is what all Chinese, wherever they may be, to this day call that area south of China, north of Australia, bounded on the west by the Indian Ocean, on the east by the Pacific. In the West it is usually more prosaically known as South-East Asia, a few people still refer to the East Indies. The northern end of the area abuts China along a long land frontier, containing a great land mass that tapers down into a peninsular that stretches south. Beyond, to the south and east lie great islands, clusters of small islands and archipelagos. The climate is tropical, still uncleared terrain and mostly jungle-clad; there are mountains, plains and great rivers; and also cities, smaller townships, industrial areas, innumerable small villages and settlements. Communications are now with some exception, generally efficient and modern. It is a mostly prosperous region although poor in parts, much of it quite densely populated, peopled by several different races, indigenous and settlers, of varying cultures, still mostly engaged in intense cultivation of the soil, also manufacturing, industry, technology, trade, both internal and external. These people are for the most part literate and basic education is widespread albeit to very varying standards. All have their own distinct traditions, art, literature, beliefs and customs and live under differing political systems. Over time the various nations of Nanyang have on occasion fought each other, have risen as seats of empire to fall again, have been attacked by outsiders, have been colonised, and have achieved independence. Now largely modernised, they constitute a driving force for change and progress in Asia.

Starting at the northern end of Nanyang are the countries that abut, or almost abut, China: Burma (now known as Myanmar), Thailand, Laos and Vietnam, with Cambodia immediately to the south. All these countries or their forerunners, have been, albeit tenuously, within the orbit of Chinese influence, direct or indirect, for up to 2,000 years. The degree and nature of this influence has of course varied greatly but it was enough to have some effect on the manners, mores and thinking of the rulers and ruling classes of these ancient kingdoms, however not on the peasantry in their remote villages and with, until very recently, such poor communications. These early links with the Han, the Chinese people, are still apparent. Down the peninsula lie the countries of the south and the islands, known to the Malays as 'the land below the wind': Malaysia, Singapore, Indonesia, Borneo and beyond, the Philippines, never in any direct contact with China, still less under any form of Chinese suzerainty however notional. Here there are no ancient links of custom, culture, religion or language. But paradoxically, the Chinese influence and presence in this region has in the past hundred or more years been profound, the direct result of Chinese economic migration in the late 19th century and after. Resentment of the Huaqiao has been stronger in these lands and assimilation harder. Either way, the Chinese Huaqiao are in Nanyang to stay, either accepted and largely integrated as in the former vassal countries near China, or still to varying degree distinct and apart, as in the lands to the south. The part the Chinese play varies considerably from country to country in the region, for example: a tiny minority in Indonesia that owns half the financial capital, the bulk of the Singapore population, the commercial hub of the region, the partly culturally absorbed large minority in Thailand.

There are historical similarities in the region. With the exception of Thailand, all were colonised by Western powers in the 19th century, indeed the Philippines, and Indonesia in part, as long ago as the 17th century. All underwent an economic boom of greatly varying proportion with the advent of rubber and other commercial crops such as palm oil and copra, grown on a large scale, the mining of tin and other minerals at the end of the 19th century, later the discovery of oil. Trade boomed, labour was needed, and the need was filled by mass immigration of labour from India and the coastal provinces of south China. After decades of growth and prosperity, earning huge revenues for their colonial masters the region was attacked and overrun by the Japanese in World War II. Apart from enormous material damage and great loss of life, the myth of European invincibility was destroyed. When the Japanese were finally defeated, the various colonial governments and businesses returned, soon to be faced by a series of struggles for independence, some bloody and protracted, some comparatively peaceful. All were successful and all the nations of the region have become fully independent, with systems of government ranging from military dictatorship to parliamentary democracy.

The very first Chinese to reach South-East Asia were a few merchant adventurers who arrived by junk, the small wooden boats with lateen sails that to this day sail the coasts of East Asia. They set out from the coastal Chinese provinces of Fujian and Guangdong and explored southwards to establish small trading settlements on the coast of what are now Vietnam, Luzon in the Philippines, the south of Sumatra, Semarang in Java and Malacca in Malaysia. A modest two-way trade with China developed: incense, spices, sandalwood, precious metals, cloth, and artefacts. The Chinese settlements did not impinge upon the local population, or hardly at all; they caused no trouble and were generally accepted. As time went by these settlement grew considerably and by the 15th century were calling points for large Chinese expeditions, led by the eunuch Admiral Zheng He, often quoted in Chinese lore, on voyages of exploration to the Indian Ocean, the Horn of Africa, and beyond. Later still, in the 19th century, trade and migration increased further. It was never accepted, encouraged, recognised or protected by the authorities in China; indeed Chinese were often forbidden to travel abroad and the Overseas Chinese settlements were totally ignored, considered to be of no interest to the Emperor and his court. This was part of the inward thinking of the ruling classes which admitted of no equal outside China, the Middle Kingdom; those who left China to live abroad did so at their peril. Meanwhile, Arab traders had long been active in the region; there was also substantial trade with India and Indian migration. The first European to reach Nanyang was the Portuguese Magellan in 1521, followed later, around 1600, by the Spanish conquest of the Philippines and its Christianisation of the people, with the exception of the Muslim Moros in the far south. This was the first colonisation by the West, followed not long after by the Dutch who conquered and occupied Java, then the other islands of the Indonesian archipelago, later to be known as the Netherlands East Indies. All the time the small Chinese communities grew and prospered.

By the early 19th century an aggressive and powerful mercantile West was trying to force an entry into China, the Middle Kingdom, and establish trading relations. All foreigners had long been deemed barbarians of various degrees, and a few were allowed to visit and pay tribute as had already been the case with the Nanyang countries for hundreds of years. This time it was different. The red-haired foreign devils, so-called by the Chinese because of their strange colouring and outlandish ways, literally blasted their way in with the first of the so-called Opium Wars and by the 1840s foreign trading posts were being established on the China mainland. This hastened the decline of what was already a faltering government, the alien Qing or Manchu dynasty which grew steadily weaker. A series of ineffectual emperors, corrupt courts and moribund government led to internal rebellion as the empire started to decay; the Taiping rebellion (1853–65) was only finally suppressed with Western help at a loss of 20 million lives. Most of these rebels came from south central China, many of them Hakkas or 'guest people' (a culture of independent people who had migrated south from north China a thousand years before, hence the name); fearing imperial retribution and to escape persecution they found their way to the eastern seaboard. From here some crossed over to Taiwan, then totally undeveloped, but most took ships south. A far smaller number trekked overland to Vietnam and Burma; their arrival in Nanyang swelled the labour market and gave a boost to the growing economies. By the latter half of the 19th century there was a growing Chinese population in or near the major ports of the region. They spoke only Chinese, had little or nothing to do with the local population and were totally self-contained communities. Most were engaged in local trade, some on agricultural holdings or working for the European-owned plantations that were beginning to be established.

What, however, really changed Nanyang forever was the discovery, in the latter part of the 19th century, that rubber trees could be grown in the region; the climate and soil were ideal. The plants, originally from South America, had been smuggled from the greenhouses of Kew Gardens in London by entrepreneurs out to Malaya. They rapidly transformed the ecology of the region and ushered in the white planter, whose heyday in Malaya was later recounted by Somerset Maugham, describing a largely British society that ran much of the economy at the beginning of the 20th century and has long since completely disappeared. Similar groups controlled the Dutch and French territories. For the most part the indigenous people: Malays, Javanese, Thais, Vietnamese and others were unwilling to change their simple and unhurried centuries old way of life and be dragooned to work on the new Western owned estates, mostly under European management. Labour was sought in India, largely Tamils from the southeast, to work as tappers and labourers. This was insufficient and contractors with their agents toured Fujian and Guangdong provinces on the eastern seaboard of China, signing up large numbers of indentured labour that were then shipped south to Singapore or other ports in the region.

Coolies, as they were called (the evocative name comes from Chinese 'ku li', bitter strength) then went to work on the estates, communally housed, poorly paid, and worked hard; organised into clans that were linked with their native village back in China. Over time a few branched out in small businesses, all mutually supporting, a very few later still made fortunes and founded commercial empires that exist to this day. Often they aroused dislike and resentment among the people near whom they had settled who regarded them as threatening outsiders and interlopers. Their acumen, hard work, clannishness, their alien beliefs, habits, customs, all aroused dislike and apprehension. This was particularly so in the countries further removed from China that had never been subjected to any such cultural influence. In Malaya, the former Dutch East Indies, now Indonesia, the Philippines, feelings sometimes ran high, exacerbated on occasion by religion. As an example, local Muslims found the Chinese liking for pork to be intolerable. Meanwhile the colonial authorities, usually in cahoots with the European estate owners tried to keep the peace; there was some segregation, and attempts made to restrict the growing Chinese influence, chiefly by discrimination in granting of business permits and facilities.

In time the Huaqiao of Nanyang, came to form an established part of the population. So did the Indians and these two alien races, principally the former, between them ran most commercial enterprises. In many cases, depending on circumstances, they were in the name of a local, a Malay, a Javanese, a Filipino purely for appearance sake, sometimes also to circumvent official restrictions. The most extreme case was in Malaya where up until the 1950s it was practically impossible to find a truly Malay business anywhere and in some states no Malay was allowed to sell his land to a non-Malay by the colonial government; the indigenous Malays were mostly not interested in commerce anyway or, if they were, business opportunities were hard to find. Traditionally there was no middle class; Malays were either peasants or aristocrats with not much in between and this applied in varying degree to other races in the region. But the coming of independence to these countries after World War II brought the recognition that such a situation was not only intolerable but also potentially dangerous. In parts of the region, legislation was introduced to promote and foster indigenous enterprise and most Chinese were far sighted enough to support it. These problems were largely confined to the culturally different countries 'below the wind', though this was not always so. One notable exception to all this was Singapore, originally an almost uninhabited island with a few Malay fisherfolk, occupied and colonised by the

British as a base for controlling the region who initiated a continual influx of Chinese who settled and made it the commercial hub of South-East Asia.

It is very hard to give a precise figure as to how many Overseas Chinese there are. In all, some 60 million Chinese live outside the boundaries of the People's Republic, nearly half of them in Hong Kong and Taiwan. The compatriots of Hong Kong – which is a Special Autonomous Region but technically not part of the People's Republic of China – number about six million, and there are some 24 million Taiwanese, citizens of the island republic, once a province of China, now independent of a China that still regards it as Chinese territory and has declared it will fight if necessary to achieve this, constituting by far the biggest and most intractable problem in the region. Neither the inhabitants of Hong Kong or Taiwan are Overseas Chinese though the former have very close connections with Nanyang. This leaves a figure of up to about 30 million Huaqiao, nearly all of whom live in Nanyang. There are also other small settlements dotted round the world, mostly dating from the 19th century, a few greatly and temporarily increased in recent years, such as Vancouver, by political uncertainty as China resumed the rule of Hong Kong. They are to be found on the west coast of the United States and Canada, in European capitals, in Oceania, Australia, in fact just about everywhere. So the Chinese of South-East Asia, number at least 25 million or more, out of the total population of the region of some 500 millions, say some 5%; proportions in each country vary enormously. In Malaysia nearly a third are Chinese, in Thailand 10%, in the Philippines less than 2%. In some countries the degrees of assimilation by the local inhabitants vary equally considerably.

The total GDP of the region as of now is estimated at around US$500 billion and growing. That of the People's Republic is about the same, perhaps more, and growing faster. Much of all investment into China is by Overseas Chinese, add in Hong Kong and it is perhaps nearly half the total. However the provenance of Hong Kong investment is often hard to define; it comes from all over, there are even mainland Chinese who bend the law and export capital to Hong Kong and then reinvest back into China, thus qualifying for all the privileges and advantages given to foreign investors. What is certain, the Chinese authorities warmly welcome all Huaqiao visiting China, they are classified as rather special tourists with the title 'Gui Guo Hua Qiao/ Returning Motherland Overseas Chinese'; they form the majority of all visitors. Many cannot speak much Mandarin, some not at all and cannot read the characters, a few cannot even use chopsticks. They are to be seen everywhere, usually in organised groups, particularly in the southeastern seaboard provinces whence their forbears came, looking up distant relations, visiting temples and monuments, bearing gifts, giving dinners in local restaurants. In fact, a frequent complaint made by Huaqiao visiting China is the expense. The Chinese government actively encourages all this; it wishes to secure the loyalty and goodwill of Chinese everywhere, plus business and investment as well if possible. There is a large Department of Overseas Chinese Affairs with branches in all the relevant provinces and everything possible is done to make the visitors feel welcome. All this is in sharp contrast to the dying days of the Chinese empire when officialdom was almost totally indifferent to Chinese abroad. The situation then altered after the foundation of the Republic in 1912, to change again during the early days of the People's Republic after 1949, when a visit to China became a political act and few travelled either way.

It is not easy to generalise about the nature of the Huaqiao as they vary so much and their backgrounds are so different; their countries of adoption range from being, in part at least, poor and backward to shining examples of 21st century life and science. But all Huaqiao have certain things in common. The overwhelming majority are descended from poor, illiterate and superstitious peasantry that eked out a living in agriculture, mostly tilling the rice padis of South-East China. They were subjects of a distant Emperor, the Son of Heaven, remote in every sense, under the more direct rule of a magistrate, usually a member of the local gentry. They were afraid of authority and rightly so, many officials were corrupt to a varying degree and took 'squeeze' (a percentage on any deal, either way) wherever they could, also were on occasion brutal and cared little for those they ruled. In time of natural disaster such as famine, flood, and drought, they starved or drowned; many of the dykes and dams had fallen into disrepair. If there was any form of internal strife, such as imperial soldiers chasing bandits, it was well to keep out of the way. Almost without exception armies of any side pillaged their way across the countryside. Often there was plague, or cholera; then they died like flies – the primitive medicines and magic incantations of the time were of course no use at all. All they had to fall back on was a mutually supporting family and far ranging clan system. There was also religion, Buddhist, Taoist, Confucian with gods and ancestors to be worshipped. Peasants prayed regularly, in the hope that some benign and generous spirits might come to their aid.

When economic disaster struck harder than usual there was desperation. Occasionally the people rebelled but that took leadership and organisation. Or they could go somewhere else. It is therefore not surprising that when, in the late 19th century, contractors and their men, often in cahoots with the local authorities who had been paid, toured villages offering jobs down in Nanyang there were many willing takers. Decisions were quickly made, usually on the same day. The man would pack a bundle of clothes, take a bag of rice and say farewell to wife and children. Women were not usually consulted on these grave matters, though in Chinese society at all levels there had always been a matriarchal influence on family matters, albeit in the background. These people then walked for several days to the coast, to an ocean they had never seen before, to be crowded on the decks or packed in the hold of a trampship whose owners extracted a fare from every passenger in earnest of future wages. They had no idea of what lay in store and only the vaguest notion of a distant land. After a cramped and lengthy voyage, coolies assembled on the docks of Singapore, Saigon, Batavia (as Jakarta was called), or Manila to begin the journey to the workplace. Occasionally it was by train, on the newly constructed railways, sometimes on foot, or a combination of both. They were dragooned into communal dwellings on the estates, in charge of overseers and started work right away. The days were long and the pay a pittance. Some however would manage to save a little and via the one or two literate members in each group would compose a letter home to go with the remittance. Early photographs of the time show these to be men who were short, tough, wiry of build, before the 1911 revolution with hair in a pigtail, later usually close cropped. They wore wide coolie hats made of bamboo, raw cotton pongee blouses, huge belts and wide black trousers, straw sandals. They formed a closed community, preserved all their customs, cooked for themselves Chinese style, spoke to each other in their regional dialect, had no contact with the local people and spoke not a word of the local language.

Their employers varied in their treatment of indentured labour, sometimes treating their men not too badly if only to get the maximum effort out of them. The then colonial governments regarded them chiefly as statistics, contributing to the growth and prosperity of the colony which looked good in the reports sent back home to Europe. There was also a legal framework of sorts that ensured a measure of law and order, policed by Europeans at arms length via a paramilitary constabulary recruited entirely from the local population. All these settlers dreamt of going home one day though very few indeed ever returned to China; they had after all left the Middle Kingdom for unknown barbarian lands. Furthermore the logistics of such a journey were daunting. The Chinese government of the day, from Emperor down to Provincial Viceroy down to Mandarins and magistrates did not bother with these people; they were of no concern to anyone but themselves. But by the end of the 19th century there were a few who cared, enlightened younger Chinese from Nanyang and China who had travelled abroad, who were part of the growing band of Chinese professionals, students and teachers, most of whom wanted reform and some, revolution. Even the successful Chinese merchants already established in the region enjoying their new found wealth would sometimes find employment or render other assistance to their unfortunate bonded compatriots.

As time went by, things got better. Some of them having worked out their contracts set up mutually supporting groups as small market gardeners, or logging, or fishing, often in settlements close to the jungle edge. Some moved to the small local towns as shopkeepers and traders, sold provisions, dealt in rice and staple crops. A few became money lenders, opened pawnshops and engaged in simple banking. Usually these ventures were successful, partly because they were mutually supportive, partly because there was little local competition. No Chinese entrepreneur was ever totally alone; if he fell ill a relative or fellow clansman would step in to help or a friend would mind the shop, if suddenly there was a disastrous lack of funds a small loan would be forthcoming. Information as to the market, prices, regulations, who to watch out for, which official to bribe, was always forthcoming. Yet not all the Huaqiao at this time were ignorant, poverty-stricken immigrant coolies, there were also a few established families and communities descended from the earlier settlers. Some of them would by dint of hard work and study qualify as accountants, get low level clerical jobs in government or the big foreign owned estates and so begin to rise. These so called 'peranakan' (Malay for native born) immigrants occasionally succeeded in getting to University to become doctors, teachers and lawyers often after great sacrifices on the part of their parents, to be repaid in time by a filial son. This was sometimes the stuff of the more modern Chinese novels and plays that began to appear at about this time. Chinese authors such as Ba Jin, Wen Yiduo and Lao She writing in the 1920s and 30s and well known in China were widely read in South-East Asia too, as was Lu Xun and his satirical essays and stories of the revolution.

Meanwhile, all this time there was little of the family life so valued by all Chinese. Few Chinese women were available for marriage, though in time the disparate proportions decreased. In the northern part of Nanyang where there was already some cultural affinity between local and immigrant, some intermarriage was possible. This was particularly so in Thailand where there came about later almost a fusion of races in some urban areas. But to the south the rigid racial barriers continued, and only relatively recently began to break down between Chinese and Malay, Chinese and Indonesian, Chinese and Filipino. These barriers were based on fear and misunderstanding. Hard-working diligent Chinese despised what they saw as idleness and lack of acumen on the part of the Malays, Indonesians and others. These in turn feared Chinese commercial aggression and were annoyed by their apparent lack of respect for their culture. Quite distinct from these communities was the extremely small proportion of very long-established Chinese groups, going back many hundreds of years, which had in part at least long since adapted to local usage and were therefore quite different from the other immigrants. They wore local costume with Chinese overtones and adornment, ate local dishes, spoke the local language, albeit with a Chinese word order and syntax, could no longer write the Chinese characters. These unique communities have long since been subsumed into the whole of modern society and speak, eat and dress like everyone else. But the more recent immigrants, be they independent arrivals, or indentured coolies, did not adapt at all for a long while. In time they learnt enough of the local language, just enough for simple contact, or work. Meanwhile, by the early 20th century, quite a few enterprising Overseas Chinese of varying background had laid the foundations of businesses that were to grow. A tiny majority of the Overseas Chinese also engaged in politics, not local, but China based, coinciding with the advent of revolution and the republic.

By the end of the 19th century it was increasingly obvious that the Manchu empire was on its last legs. Various reformers had tried and failed, so it fell to the early revolutionaries who sought to establish a republic and formed a political party dedicated to this aim. The Tungmenghui, soon to be subsumed into the Guomindang (known at the time as the Kuomintang or KMT) was led by a sincere, slightly impractical visionary Sun Yat-sen: a Cantonese medical doctor, Westernised, Christian convert, fluent in English, with dreams of a democratic state. His Three Principles, formally defined as democracy, nationalism, people's livelihoods, are still respected, albeit differently interpreted, on all sides of the Chinese political spectrum as is the man himself. Dr Sun and his followers were proscribed by the Manchu authorities and hunted, spending years abroad. When the actual rising occurred, on 10 October 1911 with the mutiny of the garrison at Wuchang, the Manchu government collapsed surprisingly quickly. There was general approbation among the Huaqiao, none of whom had any motive for supporting what had become an increasingly incompetent, feudal and alien regime. But the high hopes engendered by the Double Tenth, as the October 10 rising came to be known, were soon to be dashed. A military clique then ran north China, in the south well-meaning democrats formed a government based in Canton. There was soon intermittent civil war and for well over a decade factional fighting known as the warlord period, with no one government running the whole country. In 1925 Dr Sun died, a disappointed man, his successor, later President of China and Generalissimo, Chiang Kai-shek marched north, beat or won over the warlords, attacked his erstwhile allies the early Communists, and more or less unified China. The capital of China was established at Nanjing and many Chinese, at home and abroad, for the first time felt patriotic. This was a new feeling of nationalism, distinct from the age-old view of China as the ancestral home, with its traditional ethics and values.

The start of the Sino-Japanese war in 1937 ruined whatever chance of success the fledgling republic ever had. Feelings were aroused among the Huaqiao and a wave of sympathy for China swept through South-East Asia. Many rallied to the cause; there was an Aid China Movement, money was subscribed, a few young men went to China to join the fight. Then in 1941 came Pearl Harbor, soon after the Japanese attack on South-East Asia with a stunning series of victories. There were some South-East Asians who collaborated with the Japanese, most were passive and accepted the situation, a relative few resisted. These resisters were very largely Chinese who saw the battle as part of a wider war involving their country. When caught by the Japanese they suffered savage reprisals. Some were apolitical, some were organised and trained by the local, usually illegal and proscribed, Communist Party. In certain territories an armed and active resistance on the part of mostly Chinese Communist guerrillas, some led, trained and aided by the British and allied officers continued throughout the war, principally in Malaya and the Philippines. There was also the major war in Burma, which the British eventually won. Many local Burmese fought on the allied side, and a Chinese expeditionary force marched south to take part. When the Japanese surrendered in 1945, the colonial powers rapidly reoccupied a region in which they had, almost entirely, been discredited. All over Nanyang the Huaqiao rejoiced at victory over the aggressor.

By this time there were already resistance movements opposed to this resumption of European control, some Communist inspired and organised. These continued long after the war and fused with political movements for outright independence, mostly to peter out when the colonial powers granted their aims, some however to continue to combat the newly independent governments. They were also encouraged and supported by China, herself since the so-called Liberation of 1949 a Communist country, though actual help, men and weapons, only occurred in that northern part of Nanyang close to China. This was principally in Vietnam after 1950 where China gave massive help during both the French and the American wars; elsewhere it was not practical to do so. Rebellion in some form or other also occurred in Malaya, Indonesia, the Philippines, Burma, with sporadic unrest elsewhere and throughout Nanyang the colonial powers prepared to go, some gracefully, some not. Many Chinese of the region were involved on one side or another, though most sat on the fence, waiting to see how things would turn out. These various Communist inspired insurrections further poisoned relations between Overseas Chinese and the other races of the region and it took a generation for them to improve. Indeed vestiges of this dislike and suspicion remain in some of the southern areas of the region to this day.

Before the advent of World War II many Overseas Chinese were politicised to the extent of caring for their ancestral country and offering support. The war and subsequent political developments brought this into sharp relief. There is an old Chinese saying that comes from the 14th century classic usually known in the West as *The Water Margin*. It runs, 'Within the four seas all men are brothers' and broadly encompasses the pan-Chinese feeling all Chinese, be they mainlanders, or from Hong Kong and Taiwan, or Overseas Chinese, have for each other, no matter where they may be, or their background. All share certain attributes: pride of race and culture, affection for the ancestral country (which many of course have never seen), respect for the aged, respect for learning, the Confucian belief that the community counts for more than the individual, family ties and obligations. There is an unsentimental approach to business, politics and war. A practical approach means it is possible to change sides if circumstances so dictate. Corruption is often accepted as a way to get things done, officials are all too often venal and all believe that the networking of contacts is the best way to deal. On top of all this is interlarded the great religions of China, Confucianism, more a code than a creed with its concept of an ordered and hierarchic society, Taoism with its mystery and magic,

Buddhism, originally imported from India, with its belief in immortality. To this should be added the relatively modern injection of Christianity, all brands, also nationalism, socialism and communism. All Chinese have been subject to these various influences to greater or lesser degree. Many share a roughly similar outlook, as indeed do Overseas Chinese Huaqiao, be they market gardeners, tappers on a rubber estate, local towkays or merchants, skilful, articulate Westernised lawyers, doctors, journalists, engineers, technicians or even Christian ministers.

The Chinese have mostly preserved their separate identity and culture wherever they have settled. When Overseas Chinese go to China on a visit, they do not feel as complete strangers. Nonetheless, the differences are considerable; some of course have difficulty in coping: the freezing cold of the north in winter, the garlic breath in crowded hotel lifts, the heavy dumpling dishes, thick quilts on the bed. But all are pleased to see cultural relics at first hand, and enjoy the traditional opera and perhaps to remark that fewer and fewer of the audience are local people, instead are often mostly themselves and serried ranks of Japanese tourists armed with flash cameras. Some need interpreters, some speak Mandarin quite well, but it is very different from the rolling r's of Peking or the sibilant sounds of the Yangzi basin. They are gratified to see at first hand the great progress China is making and listen to the recital of statistics with varying degrees of attention. Many still have family ties, albeit by now remote and tenuous, almost all in Guangdong and Fujian provinces, and generally speaking feel more at home the further south they go. If business people they may be encouraged by what they have seen to consider investing some more. They know the role they play in China's development is appreciated and they find this gratifying. It is also understood that, within practical limits, China will try to protect her people overseas if help is ever needed, including even possible repatriation.

Indeed there has been a volte-face in China's attitude to the Huaqiao. When the very first settlements were established in Nanyang, it was a question of ignorance rather than indifference; the Han emperors and their officials barely knew of these early voyages of exploration, save perhaps a few travellers' tales. There were more important matters to be dealt with nearer home. It is worth remembering that at this time the two greatest empires in the world, Rome and China, barely knew of each other's existence. By the time of the Ming, say about 500 years ago, when China was just entering into a path of slow but steady decline, there was some official cognisance of settlements down south, but that was all. The view was that what went on in these barbarian lands, and what befell any Chinese who went to them, was of no concern. Early contacts with foreigners, Arab traders at Zaiton in Fujian in the 13th and 14th centuries, Portuguese on the South China coast in the late 16th century, were all dealt with by insulating them from the mainstream of Chinese life. What were in effect ghettoes were formed for foreigners who were allowed in, mainly if they were useful, to be carefully controlled and leave in due course. It was also hoped these people might benefit from their exposure to the superior benefits of Chinese civilisation. Equally, Chinese at home were periodically forbidden to travel abroad. The thinking was always, the less contact the better; indeed at one point Chinese were even forbidden to teach Chinese to foreigners, not that there were many takers: it is not surprising that the Chinese court and its ministers remained in a state of ignorance about the rest of the world. This of course included Nanyang.

By the late 19th century, when the Chinese empire was weak and in rapid decline and foreigners had moved in with a vengeance, there was a rather feeble and belated official recognition that many Chinese had settled overseas, but that was as far as it went. A Chinese Nationality Law, promulgated in 1909, stipulated any person born of a Chinese father, or of a Chinese mother where the nationality of the father was unknown or indeterminate, was a Chinese citizen, regardless of place of birth. It took the new Republic of China, proclaimed in 1912 weak, divided, riven by factional fighting between rival warlords, her overseas trade, early industry and banking almost entirely in foreign hands to take more positive steps, opening consulates in South-East Asian cities, enquiring into the welfare of the indentured labour on the estates, helping and encouraging local Chinese-owned businesses, promoting Chinese education throughout the region. After Chiang Kai-shek's reunification, by about 1930, this policy was actively pursued and every town in Nanyang with a sizeable Chinese population had an established branch of the Kuomintang. The Japanese attack on China greatly strengthened these growing bonds and they grew further during and after World War II. When Mao proclaimed the Peoples Republic in 1949 and stated that the Chinese people had stood up, the new Communist government set to work with a will to strengthen ties with all Chinese overseas. Prime Minister Zhou Enlai's dictum, ratified in 1960, stated that all Chinese might choose their allegiance: not to choose China but to choose their country of adoption did not constitute disloyalty.

Inevitably there were major problems, the colonial governments of South-East Asia were of course all anti-Communist; the Cold War was at its height and China was then firmly in the Soviet camp until the Sino-Soviet split of 1960. There were Communist-led and organised movements in various countries, Vietnam, Malaya, the Philippines, leading to wars and rebellion, all encouraged, some also aided by China throughout the 1950s, 1960s and early 1970s. Shortly after, all such support was abandoned as China sought to improve relations with the governments of Nanyang. This dramatic change was part of the great shift in Chinese policy that occurred with the advent of the Open Door in 1978, which effectively encouraged foreign business to set up in China on a massive scale. The resultant huge growth in the Chinese economy is the biggest single factor in Asia today.

3

The Tribute Bearers: Burma, Thailand, Vietnam, Cambodia, Laos

The countries in the northern part of South-East Asia are different to those of the south by virtue of a near common frontier with China. Modern Burma, now renamed Myanmar, directly abuts the Peoples Republic's Yunnan province, as does Laos; Vietnam is immediately south of Guangxi. Thailand's northern frontier is with Burma and Laos, however China is but a hundred or so miles away. Cambodia is immediately to the south and borders on Thailand, Laos and Vietnam. All these countries have from a slight to moderate degree been under Chinese influence for up to 2,000 years, their rulers sometimes sent tribute to the Emperor of China and acknowledged Chinese superiority. Travellers, merchants, pilgrims, priests, peasants, at times soldiers, have crossed over, mostly from north to south, at varying times. For reasons of difficult terrain and poor communications there has never been any large-scale overland migration; a trickle rather than a flood. Later migration was largely by sea, from China's eastern seaboard down the Vietnam coast, or further south. As elsewhere in the region, the very first Chinese settlers mostly arrived by junk during the Han dynasty, forming small coastal settlements, some to travel on further south.

That part of Vietnam that lies in the Tonkin delta near what is now Hanoi, in North Vietnam and thus close to China, then came under Chinese rule and remained so for a thousand years. This period spanned China's greatest dynasties; the Han, the Tang and ended with the Song, say around the 13th century AD. A Chinese cultural influence pervaded the region, including Annam, central Vietnam, and brought Buddhism and Confucianism, both already well established in China long before. Some of the ruling classes became sinicised in dress and custom; written Chinese language was introduced at court. The

Vietnamese king sent tribute to the emperor and continued to do so even after overthrowing Chinese rule. Just about all the other kings and rulers in this part of South-East Asia also made some gesture of subservience to the Middle Kingdom. The amount and frequency of the tribute would vary with the waxing and waning of Chinese influence and strength. Kingdoms rose and fell in the region. There was a powerful trading nation in central Vietnam and the Khmer kingdom with its celebrated capital at Angkor in Cambodia. In Southern Burma the Mon Cambodians ruled the south, also adopting Buddhism which spread throughout the whole region.

Meanwhile these nations, all of which lasted many hundreds of years had been in part influenced by Indian culture, which then diminished when the governance of India passed from Hindu to Muslim. Then in the late 13th century, when the Mongols conquered China, their armies marched as far south as Cambodia; those rulers who resisted and refused to recognise Mongol sovereignty invited fierce retribution. A period of confusion was followed by the rise of the Thai Ayuthaya kingdom which grew at the expense of the now weakened Khmer and less powerful rulers of Myanmar in Burma. A century later, the Mongols left; having as the saying went, 'seen the world from horseback', they were now a spent force in East Asia. As the millennium progressed there was continuous rivalry between the three leading powers in the region, what is now: Burma, Thailand, Vietnam. Thai and Burmese fought each other, South Vietnamese fought North, Thai and Vietnamese contested to dominate the Cambodian Khmer Kingdom. By the late 18th century despite the intermittent warfare all the kingdoms were long established, stable, powerful, well administered with an organised bureaucracy and enjoying economic self sufficiency. Having an eye to the main chance they still sent tribute to China and some Chinese cultural and commercial influence continued. There was also seaborne two-way trade and merchants and their wares crossed the border.

None of this was of much avail when the West arrived. By the beginning of World War 1 in 1914 all these countries, with the exception of Thailand, had been colonised by Western powers, as indeed were the countries in the peninsula and islands of the southern part of Nanyang. Most of the takeover took place in the latter half of the 19th century. The British, from their base in India, first invaded Burma in 1826 and in subsequent campaigns established total control, part of an overall strategy to secure the eastern approaches to India and extend British control down to Malaya and Singapore. The French extended their control from Cochin China, South Vietnam, up to Annam, they later occupied Laos and Cambodia at the end of the century. These three countries formed Indo-China and were the jewel of the French empire; less than a hundred years later they were the scene of the most spectacular defeat of a colonial power at Dien Bien Phu. The various major European colonial powers of the time were all in direct competition. The British who held Burma, and the French in Indo-China both jockeyed for power and influence in Thailand, whose astute rulers were able to steer an independent course between them and so escape being colonised, nonetheless the Thais lost four Malay states in the extreme south to the British as they occupied the Malayan peninsula.

There was also Dutch, Spanish, even American colonialism in the islands. The Americans took the Philippines from the Spanish in 1898 by force, later promised the Filipinos self-government, which they finally gave in 1945. Part of the scramble for territory, north to south, was sparked by economic and political rivalry between the European powers. Economic development and exploitation of the region, primarily for the benefit of the mother countries in Europe took place during these years, resulting among other in migration of labour to Nanyang from China and India. This principally took place in what are now Malaysia, Indonesia and the Philippines. But the ships packed with coolies called at Saigon too. There were huge estates, growing rubber, tea, copra, palm oil, roads and railways were built, and also what Kipling called in one of his poems the 'new raised tropic city'. Everything was geared to the benefit of the European colonists, some of whom made great fortunes. The already quite large Chinese population was largely indentured labour working on the Western owned plantations.

What put paid to it all, suddenly and dramatically, was the Japanese attack in 1941. Japan had little trouble occupying French Indo-China; a defeated France had a collaborationist Vichy government in nominal control of her colonies. There was not much resistance save some guerrilla activity led by the Vietnamese Nationalist Party, later to become the focus of the Vietminh movement against the French. Neither did the Thais resist, allowing a Japanese army to pass through on its way south to launch a seaborne attack on Malaya, Singapore and the Dutch East Indies, and overland west to attack Burma. Here occurred some of the most bloody and protracted fighting of the entire war. A British army, driven back to the Indian border, recovered and fought its way back to eventual victory; a Chinese army under the American General 'Vinegar Joe' Stilwell based in Yunnan province also marched south in support, the first successful military expedition out of China for 60 years. Apart from appalling destruction and loss of life the Japanese victories had two main effects: they discredited utterly the colonial powers and greatly encouraged the latent nationalism and desire for self-rule of the subject people. These various struggles for independence after 1945 were all successful and within a few years the colonial rulers had gone. The former European communities, planting, business, banking, engineering, bureaucrats, could remain, but on different terms. The entire situation was also deeply influenced by the Cold War, then at its height, as it seemed to the West that there was a Soviet attempt to take over the region by proxy. Certainly some of the national movements for liberation were, to varying degree, Communist infiltrated, even Communist led. This view was greatly exacerbated by a now belligerent China, Communist ruled since 1949, calling for liberation everywhere.

The country with the least influence on the rest of South-East Asia and that impinges little on its neighbours is Burma, the worst governed, most inaccessible and poverty stricken in the whole region. Inflation runs at over 20%, most of the population spend nearly three-quarters of their income on food and power supplies are so limited that breakdowns occur continually in all the major cities. Despite substantial natural resources, Burma remains a poor country and foreign investment is minimal. There is rampant corruption throughout government and business. It is also noted for being the second largest producer of illicit opium in the world and is a major drug supplier. There is a little light industry and prospecting for oil offshore. The main economic activity is agriculture, the logging of teak, cultivation of tobacco, jute, and cotton. Out of a population of 45 million, made up of various different but similar indigenous races: Bamar, Shan, Karen, Mon, some 2% are ethnic Chinese who, as elsewhere in South-East Asia, mostly maintain their language, customs and way of life. A larger proportion are classified as Sino-Burmese, the result of intermarriage and racial assimilation and most are Buddhists. Much of the business is cross-border trade and Chinese merchants from Yunnan and Fujian roam freely as far south as Mandalay. Most of the market capital is directly or indirectly under Huaqiao control who survive and even prosper under the present military regime. However, the Chinese have little political influence and no say in the government. Any official dealing with China was previously inhibited by Chinese government backing for the Burmese Communist Party; this changed in 1978 when Deng Xiaoping announced the Open Door policy which rapidly transformed China's overseas relations.

Before this, during World War II, the overland supply route to China, the famous Burma Road, was reopened. Nationalist Chinese troops travelled down it again in 1949, not as an army to fight as in 1944–45, but a defeated force fleeing before the advancing People's Liberation Army. In time they re-grouped on Burmese territory and established bases near the border from where they raided the ethnic minority areas of the Chinese province of Yunnan. Some penetrated further into Burma and established the infamous Golden Triangle drug-producing area, an independent enclave commanded by former Nationalist Chinese generals quite beyond control of the Burmese government. Meanwhile the British had granted independence, which was formally declared on 1 January 1948 under the first Prime Minister, U Nu. Order and unity were more or less restored fairly soon save the Karen tribesmen, who with Communist guerrilla allies controlled much of the food supplies and constituted a constant security problem. In 1962 a military coup under General Ne Win which aimed to establish a united socialist Burma with limited regional autonomy took control. There was modest economic progress and, in parts, a rise in the standard of living. Burmese culture flourished and the country distanced itself from the wars that raged in the region. In 1988, the present more repressive regime took over following a military coup d'état and has held on to power ever since. All opposition was stifled, information was censored, and communications were difficult. A nation wide election was actually held in 1990 with the National League for Democracy an outright winner. The military rulers refused to recognise the results and detained some of the democrats, in particular their leader, Aung San Suu Kyi who has since become an international figure and has been in and out of house arrest ever since despite international opprobrium. There are some slight signs of improvement now, conditions are a little better, there is less repression, a little more freedom. However, refugees still flee the country, mostly to settle in neighbouring Bangla Desh. Burma joined ASEAN, the Association of South East-Asian Nations in 1997 and there are a few signs that may encourage some possible reform.

That Thailand preserved her independence was more by good luck than good management. This was principally due to colonial rivalries in the adjoining countries allowing her rulers to somehow play one off against the other. Neither was Thailand devastated during World War II; nonetheless there was damage and loss, and like everywhere else the winds of change blew after the allied victory of 1945. Thai nationalists called themselves Muong Thai, Land of the Free, to emphasise their avoidance of colonial rule. Following some chaos a right-wing strongman, Marshal Phibul Songgram, a collaborator with the Japanese, had established military rule, which, with interruption, continued for a generation. A democratic constitution was promulgated in 1974 and civilian elected government followed; however the threat of Communist Vietnamese forces in nearby Cambodia and infiltration from Laos led to the re-establishment of a mildly repressive military dictatorship, later to be followed by a fully democratically elected government. This is in place today, as is still the monarchy, constitutional and apparently popular. GDP per capita is now over US$2,000 and growing, the annual growth rate having recently peaked at over 8%, is now 6%. Despite the setback of the Asian financial crisis of 1997 growth has resumed and confidence has been restored. The chief businesses lie in the service sector, principally tourism, which accounts for over half the total while manufacture includes vehicles, electronics, textiles, also tin mining. Agriculture includes the cultivation of rice, maize and sugar; Thailand is a major rice supplier to the region.

Out of a total population of some 60 million, nearly all Thai with a few Malays in the far south, some six million or so, say 10% are Chinese. All, apart from the Malays are Buddhist. It is hard to be precise as to proportions as so many Chinese have been assimilated through intermarriage, even many Thais and Chinese are themselves unclear as to their exact proportion of mixed ancestry. It has been estimated that practically all of Bangkok's thriving business community have some Chinese ancestry. All in all, some 80% of market capital is in Chinese hands and they control most of the economic life of the kingdom. There are long-established trading houses owned by vastly wealthy families; brokers, merchants and traders. Most of the industry is also in the hands of the Huaqiao, and they provide the capital for construction and control communications. An earlier cultural affinity with China meant that Chinese settlers had less difficulty than elsewhere in the region; many Thais originally came south from Yunnan province in the 6th century AD, and there are still discernible linguistic links. Indeed it is not always easy to distinguish the races by appearance. That said, there is still some discrimination to be found, particularly on the part of the aristocracy and the army jealous of Chinese wealth and influence. Relations with China have greatly improved since the turbulent days of Mao and the neighbouring Vietnam War when it seemed possible the whole region would fall to Communism. Thailand was the second target in the earlier Cold War-inspired American 'domino theory' which postulated that if Indo-China 'goes', the rest of the countries of the region would, one by one, rapidly follow suit. China remains a major trading partner and relations are good.

There is a long-running security problem with Burma, refugees, illegal immigrants and drugs infiltrate the long frontier between the two nations and this has led to cross-border skirmishes. The earlier problem to the far south, with Malayan Communist guerrillas, all Chinese, taking refuge on Thai territory has long disappeared. There was deterioration in relations with Cambodia over some recent anti-Thai incidents; all now settled. Throughout the Cold War Thailand was a staunch ally of the West. During the French Indo-China war however, she stood aloof. During the protracted Vietnam war she was a willing ally. Thai bases were used by the US Air Force to bomb targets in Vietnam and American troops on so-called R&R leave cavorted in Bangkok. This was when the capital began to change to a tourist attraction with a noted red light district, bars, brothels, pimps and massage houses many run by Chinese offering an increasing range of services to a growing influx of tourists. A pliant and corrupt administration quickly latched on to these opportunities for enrichment, soon turning Bangkok into the sex capital of Asia. Meanwhile Thailand continues to ally herself with the West and international relations with the US and major powers are good, including prominent and active membership of ASEAN; Thai forces have taken part in various UN peacekeeping operations around the world.

The Socialist Republic of Vietnam, over a period of some 30 years of almost continuous warfare, including defeating a European power and a global super power, has suffered more and lost more since the end of World War II than any other country in the region, probably in all Asia, with the arguable exception of Cambodia. It is still a poor country under a Communist government that rules prudently, with moderation, and has been at peace for over 20 years after a generation of warfare against major powers. Relations with neighbouring countries in the region are now quite good and the economy is developing, becoming somewhat more open to outside investment. Despite being a one-party state there is little opposition to the regime, overt or covert, partly because of the respect in which it is held for first of all defeating the French colonial rulers, then the Americans, resisting Chinese encroachment, unifying the country, maintaining peace and stability. There have been some heavily publicised crackdowns on official corruption and in the main the government is seen as doing its best for the people. A certain relaxation of dogma and adoption of more liberal policies have raised living standards and improved the quality of life; indeed the number of people living in poverty has halved in the past decade. A security apparatus still squats overall and dissidents are under surveillance. However the atmosphere is by no means oppressive.

The Vietnamese economy today is fairly sound. Exports, mainly to East Asia and Australia are growing sharply; inflation at around 5% is under control. GDP remains low at US$400 plus per head but annual growth rate of 7% is forecast. There is a minimum wage and labour conditions are mostly fair. The major industries are light manufacturing, mining as well as oil and gas production. The agricultural sector includes forestry and fishing and growing of traditional staple crops such as rice. Much of the country is jungle-covered mountain, production chiefly takes place in the great river deltas. Communications are still poor, however they are improving rapidly with a network of new roads. Controlled foreign investment is permitted but has so far been limited; it will probably increase as restrictions relax. Many of the so-called Chinese 'boat people', fled by sea to other regions in South-East Asia some years ago, have now returned and business flourishes. A by-product of a long period of peace and progress in the region has been the recent growth of tourism with the opening of resorts and the building of hotels. However tourism is nowhere near as pervasive as in Thailand, nor is the present government likely to permit the Western influence it can bring.

Some 3% of the population of Vietnam are Chinese and, as elsewhere, they control much of the free market business though not the state-controlled enterprises. A proportion have intermarried and are more or less culturally assimilated; there is presently little friction between the races. It is still remembered in Vietnam how the country was ruled by the Chinese throughout the first millennium, how the King rallied his people to expel them. Chinese influence, pervasive and continuous, continued right up to the French occupation in the 19th century, when a Chinese army, with some local Vietnamese assistance, succeeded for the first and only time in checking a large European force in the field. This was at Langson in 1884; the news of the victory took so long to reach the Chinese court that it was assumed the battle had been lost, and so more concessions were made by the Chinese. Everyone also remembers how during the wars of resistance against the French and Americans that followed World War II there was continuous massive support of arms, supplies and men from China, including even an offer of a home in China to the entire Vietnamese nation if it were ever needed. This of course was the time of China's

Mao Zedong and his Vietnamese counterpart, revered leader and patriot, Ho Chi Minh, an equally great revolutionary, sometimes disagreeing with Mao in principle, not necessarily in execution.

After the defeat of Japan it took a while before France, recovering from five years of German occupation, could re-occupy her Indo-China colonies. A Vietnamese Nationalist Party aimed at achieving freedom had already been formed and an independent republic under Ho Chi Minh was proclaimed. Negotiations as to power-sharing with the French broke down and fighting broke out in 1946. For the next eight years France did her utmost to hang on to her colony, to be finally decisively defeated by the Communist Vietminh army at the battle of Dien Bien Phu in 1954 with considerable help from regular Chinese troops: artillery, engineers, supplies. The ensuing Geneva agreement partitioned Vietnam into a (Communist) Democratic Republic in the north, with capital at Hanoi, and a Republic of Vietnam in the south, with capital at Saigon. The French surrendered all sovereignty and withdrew completely, as did the French-appointed puppet Emperor Bao Dai who had been placed on the throne as a nominal figurehead. An uneasy peace between the two sides ensued. South Vietnam's President, the autocratic Ngo Dinh Diem, like many of his countrymen a staunch Catholic, was then murdered during a military coup engineered by generals in 1963. Meanwhile Communist guerrillas, known as the Vietcong, supported by the north, were by now active in southern rural areas. All these political machinations were almost entirely Vietnamese, the local Chinese played little part. A takeover was only averted by a massive American military intervention that ended in total failure eight years later. China offered further support during these years by sending an enormous amount of supplies, much of them man-carried over the border and down the Ho Chi Minh trail. The Vietnam War long, drawn out, bloody, became the most documented, photographed, controversial and reported conflict. Following a ceasefire in 1973 and American withdrawal of troops, the two sides, North and South, failed to reach negotiated agreement. The war continued, to conclude with a total North Vietnamese victory marked by the fall of Saigon in 1975 and a diaspora of refugees fleeing the new regime. After 30 years continuous struggle the country was at last unified as the Socialist Republic of Vietnam.

Somewhat unexpectedly, soon after the war ended in 1975, relations between both Vietnamese and Huaqiao and Vietnamese and China herself deteriorated greatly, in the latter instance largely due to Vietnamese independence and unwillingness to accept Chinese leadership. By then all American economic support for South Vietnam had of course ceased. In North Vietnam there were serious crop failures; the rice lands were also under attack by the Cambodian tyrant, Pol Pot, who was indirectly supported by China. Meanwhile, a series of socialist economic measures, including the nationalisation of trade, were a disaster and there was widespread starvation. Many were badly affected, in particular the Huaqiao of Cholon (in Vietnamese known as the Hoa), the Chinese part of Saigon, some of whom lived as merchants, brokers and workers controlling the Mekong rice deltas. Meanwhile, China had already accused Vietnam of ill-treating her Huaqiao and Deng Xiaoping publicly stated China would teach Vietnam a lesson. This the Chinese then did with a massive attack preceded by a barrage of propaganda over the border in 1979, which apart from causing great damage destroyed the last stocks of rice. The Chinese attack lasted only three weeks, marking a disastrous breakdown in relations since the high point of massive support during Vietnam's great wars of resistance, only a few years before.

Vietnam's unwillingness to toe the Chinese line also marked the underlying tensions between these two ancient states whose relationship had risen and fallen for 2,000 years, plus the added pressures of international power politics, Vietnam being unequivocally part of the Soviet bloc which was by then long since at odds with China. The Vietnamese then accused their ethnic Huaqiao citizens of treachery, of siding with the enemy, of leading them to the rice stocks. They had a choice, trek north and cross into China, which many did, stay at home and starve, or leave by junk either up to Hong Kong or down to South-East Asia. Thousands of Chinese, men, women and children, called 'boat people' by the international press, packed into small, often unseaworthy, junks to set sail for various destinations, often to be denied permission to land. This tragic aftermath of the war soon subsided, in time most returned and before too long relations between the races had largely returned to the previous status quo. However since then there have been some further bones of contention which still exist between these two erstwhile allies. Although Hanoi and Beijing normalised relations in 1991, resulting in considerably increased cross-border trade, there has been a further quarrel over the South China Sea. Just before the government of South Vietnam collapsed, China seized the Paracel (Xisha) islands, Vietnamese territory, landing troops and overwhelming the garrison. Later, in 1988, China occupied islands in the Spratly (Nansha) islands, again claimed by Vietnam, and fired on Vietnamese naval vessels that resisted. A later declaration, made in 1997 by China and ASEAN, renounces the use of force to settle these claims; so far this has been upheld.

There are two further small countries in France's former Indo-China empire, Laos and Cambodia. Laos has long borders with China and all the other countries of the region, particularly Vietnam, which run, north to south, the whole length of the country; over the years there has been much two-way traffic, illicit and otherwise. Laos escaped most of the fighting during the French Indo-China War of 1946–54 and was recognised as an independent and neutral monarchy by the Geneva Agreement of 1954. Then came three-pronged civil war: royalists fighting the Communist Pathet Lao, both fighting a succession of American backed would-be warlords. In 1971 South Vietnamese forces invaded as a tactical move as the American departure began, soon to withdraw. By 1973 the Pathet Lao held the advantage and entered into a joint government with the Royalists; meanwhile the 1975 fall of Saigon with total Communist victory in Vietnam helped to ensure the establishment of a People's Democratic Republic. Laos is now under Vietnamese influence; the population of some four million or more, mainly Buddhist but one-third animists who worship nature by attributing a living soul to natural objects, continue their way of life in a mountainous land-locked country. Foreign business is chiefly with Asian neighbours, some with Western Europe. There is a little industry, both light and low tech: garment manufacture, food processing. Over half the economy is agriculture, the principal crops rice, tea, tobacco, and logging. It is not easy to be precise but only about 1% of the population are Chinese, mostly traders who cross the borders, or are settled in the capital Vientiane or the few towns. As elsewhere in the region they largely engage in business and eschew politics. Relations with the massive neighbour to the north, China, are quite good, as are those with the other abutting states.

The last of the five so-called tribute bearers is Cambodia. Having survived wars and upheavals comparatively unscathed for millennia, including World War II, and been the seat of an ancient and great civilisation, these people, known as the Khmer, suffered appallingly in the relatively brief period following the Vietnamese victory of 1975. Before then, Cambodia had been marginally involved in the French Indo-China war of 1946–54; in 1949 the ruler, the flamboyant Prince Sihanouk, had achieved a settlement with the French colonial power to lead an independent government. Full independence followed in 1955. Cambodia managed to stay out of the second Vietnam war until her neutral (and allegedly-pro Vietcong stance) provoked a US-backed South Vietnamese invasion. Sihanouk retired to live in Peking and Marshal Lon Nol took power. Despite American support the Cambodian army was thoroughly defeated by the Communist Khmer Rouge, who occupied the capital Phnom Penh in 1975. A full-scale revolution ensued, including drastic measures such as the evacuation of the entire population of Phnom Penh for re-education and forced labour in the countryside. This, and other drastic measures, plus much starvation killed nearly a quarter of the population of seven million. Meanwhile, China backed the Khmer Rouge as a counterbalance to the Soviet backing for the Vietnamese.

Shortly after, the North Vietnamese army invaded Cambodia, deposed the Khmer Rouge bloodstained leader Pol Pot and established the Khmer Peoples Republic. Things slowly got back to normal, production revived, starvation eased. Cambodian neutrality was in everyone's interest and in 1998, for the first time ever, China sent UN observers to see this had been carried out. Cambodia today remains a poor country with a third of the population below the poverty line. The infrastructure is poor but improving, agriculture has recovered, trade is growing. There is some light industry, minimal investment from abroad. The country is racked by corrupt officialdom and wholesale smuggling which makes a mockery of attempts at reform. The people are practically all Khmer, with a minority of Vietnamese and only about 1% Chinese. There is again a king and a constitution, political parties and elections. The small Chinese minority are racially quite different from the Cambodians and there has been less assimilation than in the neighbouring countries. They chiefly concentrate on business as much as possible, as elsewhere control much of the market capital while keeping clear of any political involvement. Despite China's previous support for the Khmer Rouge, relations are now quite good between the two countries.

The Chinese of Hong Kong are not of course Huaqiao and Hong Kong is not in South-East Asia; its six million inhabitants occupy a small peninsula and some islands off the Guangdong coast in South China. They constitute Nanyang's chief link with China, and vice versa. However, they consider themselves as different from their brethren on the mainland. Hong Kong had for a long time been separated from China by virtue of being a colony under direct British rule until it was handed back to China in 1997. Its citizens now belong to what is known as the SAR, Special Administrative Region of the People's Republic of China and are officially known as Gang Au Tong Bao, 'same womb compatriots'. Throughout much of her colonial past Hong Kong played a leading role in developing business on the China coast and south into Nanyang, now more than ever before. All Chinese, from all three regions, mainland, Hong Kong, Nanyang, are closely linked despite distance, dialect, culture, politics and economics and regard each other as such. Hong Kong Chinese nearly all speak Cantonese as their first language, with increasing numbers speaking Mandarin or putunghua, the lingua franca of mainland China, as well. They mostly originate from towns and villages over the border in Guangdong province, as far west as Guangxi, north to Swatow/ Shantou, south to Hainan island. A small proportion of the Hong Kong population, including a sizeable community from Shanghai, come from other parts of China. As such Hong Kong Cantonese again have much in common with many Overseas Chinese who themselves also originally came from these same areas in South China and so more or less share a common tongue.

Hong Kong's superb business facilities provide the conduit for much of the two-way flow of business between China and the rest of the world. Even during the 1960s, well before any changes in China, when the bamboo curtain was in place and the Cold War continued, when much of South-East Asia was riven by factional fighting, Hong Kong was already the 13th largest trading nation in the world. In 1945, the British reoccupied a shattered colony after a destructive Japanese occupation. In 1949, the advancing Chinese People's Liberation Army stopped short of the border; a massive influx of refugees soon gave rise to Hong Kong's economic boom making the colony the most prosperous and dynamic business centre, bar none, in East Asia. Hong Kong provided a listening post and vantage point to the self-styled 'China watchers' who would report on and analyse the situation in China. It also offered a stable base with various forms of support to the nations further south, many unstable, racked by rebellion and civil war: Indonesia, Malaya, Vietnam, the Philippines. The upheavals that also shook China at the same time, in the 1950s, 1960s and early 1970s did not materially affect Hong Kong stability and progress, though there were some extremely anxious times, in particular the riots and bomb attacks in 1967, aptly called by the then British Foreign Secretary, 'an overspill of the Cultural Revolution'.

The Chinese economic take-off, which dates from Deng Xiaoping's Open Door Policy of 1978, then set the seal on Hong Kong's future. From a pre-eminent gateway to China that already handled a growing stream of business it became the conduit for a flood, including of course the enormous growth of Chinese business with South-East Asia, most of which flowed through Hong Kong. As an example, the volume of two-way trade between Singapore and China increased seven-fold in the 1980s. Nowadays South-East Asian businesses, most of them but by no means all Chinese, who wish to deal with China in whatever sphere: import, export, banking, investment, technology transfer, consider using Hong Kong as a channel and most do. Some of course deal directly, or via Singapore which offers similar facilities but not the same direct access. The formula of government 'one country two systems' i.e. the co-existence of the totally free market economy of Hong Kong with the still partly state controlled, albeit increasingly free economy of China, suits all concerned. The same process works the other way round too; any mainland China organisation seeking outlets or business outside China will almost inevitably first try Hong Kong.

In the run up to the transfer of sovereignty back to China there was considerable anxiety among many Hong Kong Chinese as to their future. The last British Governor introduced some measures to establish a democratic system of government which was misunderstood by the Chinese government as perhaps being a left-handed way of somehow prolonging British influence. Britain's sincerity was called into question: talks went badly with each side suspicious of the other. It must be noted that ever since Hong Kong was ceded to Britain in 1841 there was never, at any time, the slightest indication that the Hong Kong public would be given a measure of democratic self-determination though a couple of years previously there had been a few modest and sensible measures to increase the local election franchise. So after much tension and abuse, to say nothing of considerable worry and expense, agreement was finally reached. The Chinese people were to be ruled indirectly by China under a formula which allowed everything to continue as before. Numerous Chinese who had emigrated as far afield as Canada and elsewhere now heaved a sigh of relief and came home. South-East Asian business joined in the still bigger boom that ensued and looks like continuing indefinitely. Meanwhile Hong Kong remains politically stable and, under the circumstances, remarkably free. Demonstrations demanding democracy are common; the people now have a taste of freedom and are not afraid to show it.

All the countries in the northern part of Nanyang, the so-called tribute bearers, have been more or less at peace for over a generation. The various wars are an increasingly distant memory. The dramatic shift in China's policy has given an enormous impetus to the economy both of the region and the ancestral country. The resultant prosperity and economic growth is reflected in increasing social stability in once divided territories. The Huaqiao are now increasingly involved in regional politics and society, as well as their traditional role as businessmen, bankers and manufacturers throughout Nanyang.

4

The 'Land Below the Wind': Malaysia, Singapore, Indonesia, the Philippines

The countries in the southern part of Nanyang, what are now Malaysia, Singapore, Indonesia and the Philippines had hardly any contact at all with China until the latter half of the 19th century when there occurred major immigration from both China and India. They were too remote, too difficult to reach; with the exception of the Malay sultanates to the far south of Thailand, at the bottom end of the Isthmus of Kra, all were separated by many miles of treacherous sea. There was thus virtually no connection at all, perhaps long ago a chance encounter with the few Chinese whose adventurous ancestors had set sail for Nanyang from the coastal provinces of China all those years ago. Some of the settlements they founded were south of what became the tribute-bearing states at Luzon in the northern Philippines, on the western coast of Malaya at Malacca, on the southern tip of Sumatra, on the northern coast of Java. Numbering on average at the most only a few hundred people, these early Han dynasty settlers kept to themselves and hardly mixed at all with the local population. A steady two-way trade developed, conducted entirely by large sailing junks, between these various parts of the region and southern China. Over time, the settlements grew, more were founded, trade increased. By the time of the Ming dynasty, say about 1,500 years later, some had become regular ports of call for the various Chinese voyages of exploration on the way west, to the Indian ocean and beyond. Later on, increasingly disturbed conditions in mid-19th century China, including the Taiping rebellion, caused a migratory wave of rebels fleeing imperial wrath. Some went to Taiwan, some trekked overland to Siam (what is now Thailand) and Tonkin while some found their way south to the islands. Later again, Western nations, chiefly the British and Dutch, rapidly colonised, or completed colonising the region. This brought in its train economic growth resulting in a major influx of indentured labour from China and southern India and so changed South-East Asia for ever.

These countries constitute all of Nanyang south and east of the former tribute-bearing countries that border on China. They are tropical, originally jungle covered, and parts have altered out of all recognition in recent years. They have been called 'negri di bawah angin' 'the land below the wind' by the Malays for hundreds of years, a phrase that still evokes the remoter parts of the region. This land includes what is now Malaysia, made up of the various sultanates on the Malayan peninsula, together with the former so called Straits Settlements of Penang and Malacca, all previously British colonies. There is the city state of Singapore. To the west and south lies the huge Indonesian archipelago, Sumatra, Java, Sulawesi, Kalimantan and myriads of islands, large and small; also the Borneo territories of Sabah and Sarawak. These border on the small independent oil rich sultanate of Brunei. Last come the Philippines, again a massive archipelago stretching north to south: Luzon, Visaya, Mindanao. All these lands with different languages, albeit often with largely similar roots, ruled in feudal fashion by princes, sultans and rajahs were entirely self-sufficient and had little to do with the outside world. Their way of life remained unchanged for centuries.

By about the time of the end of the Tang dynasty, say a thousand or more years ago, when power struggles were already taking place on the South-East Asian mainland, the same process began in the islands to the south. In Sumatra the powerful Sriwijaya Kingdom vied with the Sailendra Kingdom on Java to monopolise the inter-regional trade, in time to be challenged by merchants from southern India. Piracy increased and spread through the islands, local chieftains raided neighbouring territories. Later, in the 14th century, what was to become the paramount dynasty, the Madjpahit of Java, came to power. At this time, Indian Hindu cultural influence began to wane, roughly coinciding with Mongol incursions south of China which encouraged the growth of Buddhism in the tribute bearing states. In the 'land below the wind' Islam had already been long since introduced by Arab Sufi traders and in time much of the region was converted, though pockets of Hinduism remained. Meanwhile Malacca emerged as the premier trade emporium in the region, ships sailed up and down and round the coasts, over to Sumatra, down through the clusters of small islands to Java, and beyond. For a very long time there was a general political, economic, cultural status quo. Occasionally there was trouble, but for the most part the various peoples: Malays, Sundanese, Javanese, Balinese, Moros, Visayans, Bajaus and numerous minorities lived at peace with each other.

The first Europeans reached Nanyang in the early 16th century; Portuguese navigators who as well as landing in the Philippines also later founded Macao off the Chinese coast, thus laying the foundations of a Portuguese eastern empire that included Malacca on the Malayan coast, and Timor in the Indonesian archipelago. Spain, then at the peak of her power, added to her South American colonies by occupying Luzon, establishing a capital at Manila from where Spanish rule extended over the whole Philippine archipelago. Spanish colonisation was cultural as well as economic and political; a large proportion of the local population were converted to Christianity. To this day most Filipinos are Roman Catholic and bear a Spanish sounding name, the chief exception are the Muslim Moros, to the far south, who are in a near permanent state of rebellion. Soon after, in 1601, the Dutch began their occupation of Java and in time came to control most of what is now Indonesia. This rule was efficient, and like the other colonial regions, unabashedly exploitative; total control over remoter parts however was not achieved until the beginning of the 20th century. A while later the British came on the scene, to occupy Manila briefly during a mid 18th century war with France and Spain, later in 1819 to annex Singapore, then Malacca in 1824, having already temporarily taken over part of the Netherlands East Indies during the Napoleonic Wars. British power, based on her Indian empire, came to extend to Burma, then down to Malaya, on to Borneo. The coastal areas and the few towns of the region were now all flying someone's flag. Deep in the interior, nothing had changed.

An aggressive mercantile West had forced its way into China in the early 19th century. The same governments, to greater or lesser degree, started to take over the as yet uncolonised part of southern Nanyang at the same time. This mission was variously described in the West as 'Pax Britannica' or 'la mission civilatrice'; the basic idea being that the West was doing these people a favour and that they should be accordingly grateful. Sometimes, depending on the power, the rule was harsh, sometimes comparatively mild with a genuine, albeit patronising, concern for the ruled. The British ruled Singapore, Malacca and Penang as a direct colony known as the Straits Settlements, the Malayan mainland via the FMS, Federated Malay States, and the Unfederated Malay States by indirect rule. In all cases the local native ruler, usually a Sultan, would be flanked by a British adviser in whites and solar topee.

The locals had some very limited say, and the eventual possibility of self-rule in the far distant future was accepted. The Dutch colonists of the day were painstaking and thorough, learning to speak Malay far better than did most English; many, particularly planters, married local women, something British prejudice largely eschewed. Yet the resultant mixed blood communities mostly turned against Holland when the time for independence came in Indonesia. In remoter parts, such as Borneo, individual adventurers carved out colonies, the most notable Rajah Brooke in Sarawak in 1846, later to be subsumed into British rule. His system of rule through local Malay chieftains, Dyak headhunters and the so called Kapitan Chinas who represented the Chinese settlers worked well in a territory entirely without roads. Perhaps the most famous colonist of all was Stamford Raffles, gifted administrator, visionary, naturalist, collector, scholar, who more or less single-handedly ran the entire British presence in the early years of the 19th century, founding the colony of Singapore in 1819, having already led a British occupation of Java and South Sumatra during the Napoleonic Wars. He did all this while still in his thirties, to die not long after in England following a long and painful illness, abandoned by his employers, the East India Company, and in debt.

By the end of the 19th century the whole region was colonised. Europeans occupied all important administrative posts without exception, headed the big firms, managed the estates, officered the local levies, and sat in judgement in the courts. Relations between colonial powers were usually good, albeit affected by how things were going back home. One unusual development which greatly affected part of the region was the Spanish-American war over Cuba resulting in American victory and takeover of the Philippines, marked by a naval battle in Manila Bay in 1898 during which Admiral Dewey sank the Spanish fleet. The Filipinos were promised self-government, which they finally attained after World War II. The Dutch empire, out of all proportion to the size of Holland to which it made an enormous economic contribution, was by far the biggest. It was generally peaceful with periodic local rebellions, such as Aceh in North Sumatra (which lasted until very recently), plus some more passive resistance in Bali and East Java which lasted until the 1930s. The Americans took over the Spanish task of pacifying the Moro rebels on Mindanao. The British put down minor disturbances in Borneo and the Malayan hinterland. All joined to try and quell the piracy which flourished throughout. Then came the dramatic discovery that rubber could be grown in the region and the economy took another leap forward. The boom that followed was hardly affected by World War I which did not touch the region at all, save the young men who went home to fight. European planters, Chinese merchants, bankers, traders, all made fortunes. The officials and administrators led what was at the time sometimes called the life of Riley in the cities, or drink sodden loneliness in up-country stations. The Chinese immigrant labour force, after much initial suffering, settled into their new lives.

World War II came abruptly to the region with the Japanese attack on Hong Kong and soon after the Philippine capital Manila; the former fell on Christmas Day 1941, a remnant of American troops and Filipino irregulars held out on Corregidor near Manila for several months. Passing through what was Indo-China, then Thailand, a Japanese army attacked Malaya, rapidly advanced down the peninsula and so over the Causeway to the great bastion of Singapore, the hub of Southern Nanyang, which to the consternation of Britain and her allies, surrendered soon after. Meanwhile another Japanese army had struck west into Burma. Early in 1942 Japanese troops landed on Sumatra and Java, and it was now the turn of the Netherlands East Indies. The outnumbered Dutch troops and the local levies were no match for the invader and Japan soon controlled the entire archipelago. By now the whole of South-East Asia from the Burma-Indian border to New Guinea had passed under Japanese control. A few of the local population, particularly those involved in the nascent independence movements, welcomed the Japanese, most sat on the fence. Not many resisted after the Japanese attack. European residents and surrendered allied troops were herded into prison camps under the most shocking conditions. The economy of the region was organised to supply Japanese needs and bolster the Japanese war effort. There was much suffering and general destruction; the occupying forces were brutal and given to plunder and rapine.

There was some local organised resistance to the Japanese, principally on the part of Overseas Chinese in the region who already regarded them as the enemy that had attacked China. In the Philippines resistance continued in some of the islands, conducted by both Filipino and Chinese guerrillas, supported by British, Australian and American submarines, later to link up with the Americans when they landed in 1944. In Indonesia there was little armed resistance save some sporadic attack on military installations. In Malaya it was different. A few British officers linked up with Chinese members of the Malayan Communist Party who had meanwhile formed the Malayan Peoples Anti-Japanese army and went deep into the jungle, emerging occasionally to attack enemy outposts and convoys. For three and a half years they served without respite, under extremely difficult conditions, no medical attention for wounds or the debilitating jungle fevers, often racked with malaria, half starved, nor receiving any form of outside support, to emerge victorious at the end. Whenever the Chinese resistance was captured by the Japanese, whether jungle guerrilla, saboteur, supplier of provisions, carrier of news, the punishment was usually rapid execution by beheading. When the war finally ended and the allied powers returned, the British to Singapore and Malaya, the Dutch to Indonesia, the Americans to the Philippines, most believed that things would go on as before. As the bands played on the Singapore Padang at the victory parade and the soldiers marched past, including the Chinese guerrillas who limped to keep time to the unaccustomed martial music, it was not appreciated that nothing would ever be the same again.

Some of the colonial administrators took time to get back in force. The British promptly reoccupied all former territories, shipped Japanese prisoners of war back to Japan, put war criminals and collaborators on trial, set about clearing up the mess, re-establishing the framework of colonial rule. The starving emaciated scarecrows that were liberated from the Japanese camps were rehabilitated and shipped home. In other colonial territories such as Indonesia there was an interregnum while the Dutch, having been occupied by the Germans throughout the war, were unable to organise a force to re-occupy for several months. British and Indian forces were sent to Palembang in Sumatra, Batavia and Surabaya in Java to contain the situation. In some cases Indonesian nationalists, later to fight the Dutch, had already taken over. Differing attitudes are illustrated in that the local British commander in Palembang in Sumatra organised football matches between British soldiers and Indonesian nationalists; when the Dutch finally arrived the first thing their commander did was stop the games. A similar situation also existed at this time in France's former Indo-China empire where it was months before the French returned in any number. There was no such difficulty in the Philippines, the Americans returned on totally equal terms, handing over power as quickly as practicable. Minor colonial powers such as Portugal, still occupying East Timor, had been neutral throughout the war and were quite unaffected. The major powers had been discredited by their defeat and few realised how little time was left, and how soon change would come. Alone among the victorious allies the Americans had no wish to prolong any form of imperial rule.

Malaysia combines the former Federation of Malaya, previously the British-run Federated and Unfederated Malay States and the Straits settlements, together with the Borneo territories of Sabah and Sarawak. This new country came into being only in 1963 and in recent years has both thrived and prospered. Malaysia is now stable and at peace with its neighbours. Out of a population of some 25 million about a third are Chinese, the rest are mostly Malay and there is a substantial Indian minority; after many years of racial tension a formula for government has evolved that suits both Chinese business acumen and Malay political aspirations. Standards of living are high, the GDP per capita is now over US$4,000, second only to Singapore in the region. Industry is modern and grows apace: electronics, oil, chemicals, textiles, and timber. Communications are excellent, the commercial infrastructure is modern and efficient. The mainstay of the economy is still agriculture, either smallholdings or large estates – rubber, copra, palm oil. The population is literate; the national language is Malay (officially known as Bahasa Malaysia) which is spoken by all while English is extremely widespread and serves as the chief language for business. The various Malay states still have their ruling Sultans who take it in turn to be King of Malaysia, nominal head of an elected government. Peninsula Malaya is part jungle, now much developed and criss-crossed with roads. What is called East Malaysia, the Borneo territories, is also much developed in the coastal areas, jungle-clad inland. This is the country the British first took over in the late 19th century and ruled until 1942, to resume their rule again in 1945.

For many years Malaysia has been governed by three main racial-based political parties that exist within the framework of a national coalition known as the Barisan Nasional. The first is the United Malay National Organisation (UMNO) which represents Malay nationalism; the second is the Malayan Chinese Association (MCA) which represents Chinese economic strength; and the third is the Malayan Indian Association (MIC) which protects the interests of the substantial Indian minority. However, whereas in all other parts of Nanyang the Chinese are in a far smaller minority, in Malaysia they are nearly a third of the population and the possibilities of racial tension and strife were, until relatively recently, considerable. Long ago, the British kept the races apart and protected the Malays from Chinese economic domination; this sort of policy is no longer possible. Some years after independence the government introduced a New Economic Policy that has set in train a major realignment of the economy by encouraging Malay business. This policy of positive discrimination has worked, and the Malay businessman is now as frequent as he was once rare. The Chinese were farsighted enough to see such a solution was essential and to everyone's benefit; *'bumiputra'*, Malay for sons of the soil, and their frequent Chinese partners are now everywhere. Gone are the days when any business with a Malay name was only a front and practically no Malay middle class existed. Gone too, with occasional exception, are the racial rivalries between Malay and Chinese. China herself is no longer regarded with hostility and suspicion, a legacy of her support for the Communist insurgents during the Emergency (1948–60) and relations are now quite good. Actual diplomatic relations between the two countries were established as long ago as 1970, remaining moribund until China's Open Door Policy came into effect. Malaysia enjoys excellent foreign relations worldwide and belongs to all the relevant organisations, in particular ASEAN of which she is a founder member.

In the summer of 1948 the almost entirely Chinese Malayan Communist Party led by guerrilla leader Chin Peng presented a series of demands to the British calling for the establishment of a Socialist state; these were rapidly rejected and a rebellion ensued that was to last 12 years and cause much loss and damage. A large guerrilla force, almost entirely Chinese, some of them veterans of the World War II anti-Japanese resistance, formed the Malayan Peoples Liberation army which from a series of bases, mostly deep in the jungle, commenced operations with the avowed aim of overthrowing British rule. Arms were readily available from supplies hidden in caches at war's end, or supplemented by raids on police posts. A support organisation, the Min Yuen, provided supplies, back-up and recruits. Attacks spread rapidly over much of the country: planters were murdered, estates attacked, rubber trees slashed; there were road ambushes, train derailments, raids on villages and small towns, incidents everywhere. On the whole, areas with a high incidence of Chinese population and thus offering possibilities of support were more likely to be attacked or occupied by the bandits as they were then called (later they were renamed with the more politically correct title of CTs, Communist Terrorists). Most of the Huaqiao business community stayed aloof at the outset of the rising; increasing numbers came to support the government. The so-called white areas which were predominantly Malay and thus hostile to the rebels, were more often left alone. The lowest point for the British was the ambush and murder in June 1950, of the High Commissioner of the Federation, Sir Henry Gurney, in broad daylight, en route to his residence.

Meanwhile the British had reacted with all due speed, declaring a State of Emergency and sending out troops from the UK, at the same time greatly expanding local forces. These were almost entirely Malay who flocked to the colours to fight a Chinese enemy. There were British infantry battalions and armoured car regiments, the famous Gurkhas, Special Forces, police jungle squads, Commonwealth troops from Australia, New Zealand, Fiji, Rhodesia, patrolling deep into the jungle often for days or weeks on end, organising road convoys, guarding trains, establishing safe perimeters around settlements liable to attack. In time an efficient intelligence network made the enemy easier to find and draconian laws were promulgated; the illegal possession of only one round of ammunition could carry the death penalty. As during the war, the Communist Chinese fought on bravely, without medical succour or supplies, often short of food and ammunition, enduring months and years of rigorous conditions without respite. What began to turn the tide was a massive resettlement programme that moved vulnerable Chinese settlements near the jungle edge where they were prey to CT attack, to stockaded villages under guard, thus denying food and supplies to the enemy. At the same time, a campaign to win the 'hearts and minds' of the people of all races, in the words of the eventually victorious British supremo Field Marshal Sir Gerald Templer, was launched. In time the tide turned, the CTs began surrendering, the British were winning. In 1957 Malaya was granted complete independence by Britain, its first leader a Malay aristocrat, trained as a barrister, Tunku Abdul Rahman. This refuted any last arguments for rebellion and in 1960 the Emergency was officially over.

The next trial of strength came in 1963 when Indonesia, still ruled by the eccentric, flamboyant Sukarno, set in train a campaign to destabilise the new nation to their north. This confrontation, or 'Konfrontasi' as it was called, was brought about by Indonesian suspicion that the British still exercised colonial power, albeit indirectly, and that this therefore was an example of necolim, or neo-colonialism. Indonesian commandos raided targets on the Malaysian mainland, also attacked Singapore. There were incidents at sea and fears of a full-scale invasion. Physical losses were moderate, but the effect on confidence, social, political, business, was most considerable. Fortunately the whole rather pointless exercise came to an end three years later with the fall of Sukarno and regime change in Jakarta. This campaign, and the far more serious Emergency that preceded it, were both supported by China but with encouragement only, no actual support or intervention in any way. Then in 1969, serious race riots resulting in many deaths, erupted in the capital, Kuala Lumpur; they principally resulted from Malay fears of Chinese economic domination. Martial law was imposed and democracy suspended for two years; it was after this that the Malaysian government introduced its new policy which laid the basis for an economic and social balance between the races. There has been no serious racial strife since.

Singapore was not directly affected by the Malayan emergency insomuch as there were no direct attacks on the territory. It continued as a huge military base supplying all the facilities the British security forces needed to prosecute the jungle war: training grounds, ammunition depots, signal centres, artillery ranges, a great port for the navy, airfields for the RAF. Security was extremely high and all the emergency regulations applied; there was little overt Communist activity in the crowded streets. About the main disruption was an ugly riot with some religious overtones among the Malay minority in 1950, massive strikes and labour unrest a few years later. The chief reminder of the war to the north was the young British soldiers down on leave from jungle operations drinking beer in the bars and amusements parks. Meanwhile business continued to grow and the maritime roads south of the island were full of shipping from all over the world. As Malaya became independent in 1957, so Singapore followed in 1959 with internal self government, followed by total independence in 1965. Singapore joined the new Malaysia in 1963, to leave two years later as an independent island republic and has been economically successful ever since. The downturn caused by British military withdrawal was quickly surmounted and the economy grew apace for 30 years. The Asian financial crisis was also skilfully handled by government support on the stock market for local investors. Growth continues at 7% and the GDP per capita is by far the highest in the region. The Singapore population enjoys a higher standard of education than anywhere else in Asia with the possible exception of Japan.

All the great cities throughout the region have what is called a Chinatown, a part that is inhabited and run by Chinese, full of Chinese shops, businesses, markets and people. There are Chinese signs everywhere, traditional music wailing from radios and loudspeakers, a whiff of joss from a wayside store, street vendors, cooked food stalls, coolies carrying loads at a shuffling trot, restaurants, tea houses, tailors sitting cross legged in shop fronts, craftsmen plying their trade. As dusk falls you can often hear the crash of mah-jong tiles, see clouds of steam from kettles and cooking pots, smell smoke from open fires and the various types of cooking. Beggars, pimps, labourers, office workers, housewives, priests, jostle each other on the crowded pavements. The difference with Singapore is that it is all Chinatown; it is a predominantly Chinese city with the exception of a Malay district. Other races, Indians in particular are of course to be found in many parts but much in the minority. Another difference is that Singapore, unlike the other Chinatowns of Nanyang is totally modern, extremely efficient, well run, orderly, law abiding and antiseptically clean. A vast long-term government project has housed practically the entire labour force in high-rise blocks. An efficient public transport system has put many of the taxis and trishaws (bicycle rickshaws) out of business. Public order is maintained by an efficient police force, part of a municipal organisation that runs the city both comprehensively and intrusively. The stories about regulations proscribing smoking, long hair and chewing gum are true. Throughout the city there are great modern blocks: residential, office, banking, government. Few old buildings remain; those that do are carefully preserved. It was not always so. In the mid 20th century Singapore consisted mostly of four-storey pre-war buildings fronting on to covered walkways, some with a deep monsoon drain running alongside. Streets were often by category of occupation: one for carpenters, one for metalworkers, tailors, rice merchants and so on. It was already a great city with all the bustle and vigour of an oriental entrepot. The coming of self-government, readily granted by the British, brought the realisation of a potentially difficult position. The Malayan emergency was only just over, Indonesia was becoming hostile. Soon after China was plunged into the Cultural Revolution and the Vietnam War raged. Singapore sought to create a stable base in an unstable Asia.

The ruling Peoples' Action Party has been in power ever since independence and holds practically all the elected seats; the present Prime Minister is the son of Singapore's first leader, Lee Kuan Yew. The population of some three million is overwhelmingly Chinese, mostly of Hokkien origin; many speak Mandarin and English is extremely widespread. The authoritarian rule imposed, with its strict regulations as to deportment and citizenship and its concept of Asian value is generally accepted. As a major financial centre with the most up to date communications, Singapore continues as the hub of the region and for some, a second gateway to China. Industry flourishes, principally electronics, chemicals, rubber, shipyards. Some years ago the government under Lee Kuan Yew made the farsighted decision to force up the minimum wage by 20%, thus ensuring industry moved rapidly into the high-tech sector; the workforce is better paid than any other in the region. Singapore believes in free trade and plays a full part in all the relevant international organisations such as the UN and the World Trade Organisation, also of course ASEAN. Any threat of Communist subversion has long since disappeared, as has any threat from Indonesia. Relations with Malaysia, just over the causeway that links the island to the mainland, are close. Relations with China are now far better; although actual diplomatic recognition did not occur until 1990 by which time trade was already booming. China has expressed admiration for Singaporean efficiency and the reservations of a generation ago have very largely gone. Singapore is punctilious in her membership of all relevant international bodies.

The small Sultanate of Brunei on the Borneo coast lies between the Malaysian states of Sarawak and Sabah. Originally a British protectorate, it achieved full independence in 1971. Its mostly Malay people live entirely off the proceeds of the oil that is drilled in the region and there is no poverty; they and their ruler are far and away the richest in resources in the area. Brunei has managed to survive independently and has not been subsumed by any of its large neighbours; it is entirely geared to oil, has no politics worth the name and plays no significant part in the regions affairs. Its rulers invest heavily overseas and certain major Chinese businesses use it both as a haven and as a base. The rule is autocratic; the Sultan is not only Head of State, but also Prime Minister, Defence Minister and Finance Minister. GDP per capita at US$13,000 is high; the Chinese minority of about a sixth of the population control much of the market capital. Relations with neighbouring states are good and Brunei belongs to all the usual international bodies. A heavily subsidised government that provides continual social benefits to the people has obviated any potential unrest. It is in everyone's interest, including that of the Huaqiao, to preserve this status quo.

The Republic of Indonesia is noted for its size, its diversity, its many races and languages, its beautiful scenery, fertile soil, romantic appeal, poverty, official corruption, inequality and frequent misrule. About 215 million people, 3% of whom are of Chinese descent live on the chain of islands that stretches from Sabang in north Sumatra to the west, right across to Merauke on the border between Irian Jaya and Papua New Guinea to the east. Nearly half the population are Javanese who dominate the social and political scene, then there are Sundanese, Madurese, Malays, Moluccans, Balinese, all speaking regional languages; there are also numerous different dialects. Just about all Indonesians, despite often poor communications and inadequate formal schooling speak the national language, Bahasa Indonesia, based on Malay. The majority, well over 90%, are Muslims with a substantial Hindu minority centred on Bali, and Christians in Molucca. The countryside varies from volcanic mountain ranges to jungle to terraced padi fields on hillsides, to great rivers; there is a fairly efficient railway network, inter island shipping, airfields, roads. Much of the population lives in small villages, eking out a living at subsistence level, sometimes so poor they live in a virtually no money economy. Most are employed in agriculture either on big estates growing tea, coffee, rubber, palm oil or village smallholdings. There are also huge cities; Jakarta the capital has a population of 16 million and some of the worst slums to be found anywhere. Most of the industry abuts the cities and provides employment, usually under poor conditions. There is cotton spinning, garment manufacture, plastics, toy manufacturing. By far the biggest earner is oil exploration offshore. Not surprisingly the GDP per capita is low, about US$400 but there is now steady growth and inflation, previously the bane of the economy, is well under control. There remains a great gap between rich and poor and some Indonesians say the country is too big and too fragmented and so too difficult to rule as one nation.

The Partai Nasional Indonesia (PNI) was already unsuccessfully seeking independence from Dutch rule well before the war. Many welcomed the Japanese as liberators and collaborated actively with the conquerors. In 1945 Merdeka, freedom, was proclaimed and the new national flag was raised; fighting soon broke out as the Dutch troops sent out from Holland disembarked at Batavia (as Jakarta was then called). A truce was brokered which did not last and in 1947 the Dutch launched a so-called police action in Java and Sumatra to seek out and destroy what was already called the TNI (Tentara Nasional Indonesia), the Indonesian National Army. Then followed the second police action in 1948; the Netherlands airforce bombed the rebel capital at Jogjakarta and re-established control over much of Java. Not all Indonesians supported the rebels, troops from Ambon, once known as the Spice Islands, fought for Holland and there were colourful adventurers such as Turko Westerling who won some stunning victories such as capturing Bandung with 10,000 men in 1948. But general world disapproval, UN opposition, the sheer magnitude of the task and the limits of her strength caused Holland to seek peace. At the end of 1949 Indonesia was declared an independent unitary state. Only West New Guinea, what was later renamed Irian Jaya, remained in Dutch hands, to be returned later in 1963. Throughout the entire struggle the rebel movement was led by Sukarno who, for a while at least, succeeded in largely unifying his country which then settled down to an uneasy peace. Islamic terrorists, the Darul Islam who sought a theocratic Muslim state, were active in West Java. In 1957 a separatist movement, angered by Javanese domination of political and military power, took up arms in Sumatra, later spreading to Molucca, and was only subdued with considerable difficulty. Throughout these troubles the Huaqiao played little part.

Sukarno called his rule guided democracy and to the alarm of the Western powers flirted with the then Soviet bloc, particularly Mao's China. The conference to end the Indo-China war and settle the region was held at Bandung in Java in 1955 where the concept of non-alignment was declared and in that same year a treaty of dual nationality with China (actually ratified in 1960) was signed. This solved a far-reaching and very long-standing problem. Hitherto all Chinese, no matter where, were considered to be citizens of China; the Chinese premier, Zhou Enlai agreed that henceforth Chinese could bear allegiance to the country of their adoption without being seen as disloyal to the mother country. By this time Communist influence in Indonesia was strong and growing, it was much resented by the military in particular. Meanwhile the Huaqiao, some long-established since the early 19th century or before, have survived intermittent persecution in various forms ever since the republic was founded. Glodok, the Chinese quarter of Jakarta was burned down; Chinese businesses and shops pillaged; Chinese schools closed; and books and newspapers banned. Chinese have sometimes been hunted down by an army which still, on occasion, regards them with dislike and suspicion. However the situation has since much improved though to this day there remains occasional anti-Chinese discrimination. Over the years many a Chinese shopkeeper has been robbed and many a Chinese restaurant has fed armed soldiers for nothing. Yet most of this 3% of the population are accepted, live at peace with their neighbours and conduct their business. As elsewhere in Nanyang they exert an economic influence out of all proportion to their size, controlling some 60% of the financial capital.

Sukarno's erratic policy of Konfrontasi against Malaysia, which started in 1963, was overtaken by events. In 1965, the then-powerful PKI (Partai Komunis Indonesia) the Indonesian Communist Party attempted a coup, aided by secret arms shipments allegedly from China. A counter-coup, led by army generals, then followed and was soon successful. Sukarno was ousted, General Suharto became President and an amalgam of military and so-called technocrats, civilian experts, took over the government. The ruling party was named Golkar, a meaningless title meaning functional groups, and rubber stamped the harsh measures of their backers. The Communist Party was proscribed, its members hunted down, many were slaughtered, as were numerous Chinese even on grounds of race alone. There were rumours of rivers that ran with blood, of killings of suspected Party members on the flimsiest of evidence, of how sometimes a Chinese accent when speaking Indonesian was enough to excite hostility. The new government broke all diplomatic links with China, ceased action against Malaysia, firmly joined the Western camp, and encouraged foreign investment in an economy that was on the verge of total collapse. Then followed years of stability and progress, albeit one sided. Most generals had a Chinese business *tjukong,* literally pillar, who provided funds and received support in return. Many of them would take Indonesian names, often those used by Javanese aristocrats, to the annoyance or amusement of their masters. Corruption and nepotism spread throughout government everywhere. Jajasans or institutes, ostensibly charitable, but in reality vehicles for tax evasion were established throughout the major cities. Corrupt officials and Chinese bankers and businessmen made huge fortunes.

In 1975 the former Portuguese colony of East Timor was given independence, after hundreds of years of Portuguese rule. It was rapidly occupied by the Indonesian army who moved in on the pretext of protecting the territory from a Communist takeover. A bloody and protracted civil war ensued in which many thousands of people were killed, perhaps 10% of the population; the territory was later placed under UN supervision. The small Chinese minority kept out of the fighting as much as possible, though, as elsewhere, some of the businesses were robbed and ransacked by the military. By this time the Suharto government was famously corrupt and top-heavy, the Asian financial crisis of 1997 destroyed confidence; the President was unsuccessfully indicted for his, and his family's greed and dishonesty. In 1999 there occurred the first free and democratic election held since 1955; the new President attempted some overdue reforms, to be impeached himself for some financial scandal. Then came Megawati Sukarnoputri, daughter of Sukarno himself, and most recently President Bambang Yudhoyono, once again an army general with essential army backing. Meanwhile there is violence in Kalimantan, an uneasy peace reigns in Aceh, ravaged by the tsunami, some fighting in Molucca and terrorist bombs in Bali. The biggest and most intractable problem of all is the growing poverty of a large proportion of the people. At least problems are recognised and the government, albeit slowly, is backing reform. Meanwhile Indonesia continues to fulfil her international obligations by belonging to the usual international and regional organisations in particular as a big oil supplier, OPEC, also the Asian Development Bank, ASEAN and so forth.

The Philippines did not have to fight for an independent democracy, but had to fight to keep it. Immediately after the Japanese surrender, the Americans reoccupied, honoured their long-standing promise of self-government; a constitution modelled on American lines was ratified the following year. Part of the deal was maintenance of the great bases at Clark field (air force) and Subic Bay (navy). Much of the country, particularly Luzon, had been devastated and the new government's first task was reconstruction. At the same time the Communist Hukbalahap, originally the Anti-Japanese Peoples Liberation Army, many of whose members were Chinese, a guerrilla force that had resisted the Japanese during the war, rose in rebellion and within a few months controlled much of Luzon. By 1950 they posed a serious threat to the government and a vigorous military campaign, supported and encouraged by the United States ensued. By 1954 the situation was restored. The Huks, as they were known, received encouragement from China; however as with the Malayan emergency, that was all. Meanwhile the country recovered economically though most people remained poor; stability and prosperity for a minority ensued. A series of right-wing governments, democratically albeit corruptly elected followed until 1965 when a repressive dictatorship under Marcos came to power. The constitution was rewritten, the press was gagged, dissenters imprisoned. This lasted for 21 years, to be overthrown by a liberal-inspired insurrection led by Cory Aquino, widow of a popular hero who had been previously gunned down by security thugs. The Aquino government instituted necessary reforms but was prey to endless attempts at a takeover by right-wing elements; no fewer than ten plots were uncovered. Meanwhile after protracted negotiations an agreement was negotiated in 1991 for the Americans to withdraw from their bases and they were soon gone.

There are over 80 million Filipinos including a small Chinese minority of 2%. Most of the population speak fluent accented English as well as their native Tagalog in Luzon, Visayan in the central islands, Moro in Mindanao. Many of the Chinese are Catholic, the rest Buddhist. Nearly all Filipinos are of a similar racial stock to that of the Malays and Indonesians and their various languages have common roots. There is also a small upper class with varying proportions of Spanish blood called *mestizos*. Filipino society tends to be hierarchical; many prominent political figures are related to each other. As with Indonesia the land, much of it beautiful, is a myriad of islands, large and small, jungle covered, many mountainous, linked by regular island ferries. Life in the barrios or villages is desperately poor for most and many ordinary people travel abroad to seek work. Filipino women provide a large proportion of domestic help in Hong Kong and are to be found all over the world. The small Chinese minority, as elsewhere in the region, controls over half the market capital. However, there is seldom any racial tension, many have married local people and are fully accepted; a large proportion of merchants and traders in major cities are of mixed race. Filipino industry has attracted quite a lot of foreign investment and is growing; principally electronics, textiles, chemicals and copper mining. Likewise agriculture, the mainstay of much of the economy: chief crops are rice, maize and sugar cane. The former is grown all over the country and you can see terraced padi fields on most hillsides. The GDP per capita is just over US$1,000 of which 10% flows from wages earned working overseas. External trade is principally with the US, Japan and Singapore, also Nanyang, and overseas relations are generally good. There is now a slight improvement in the economy and ordinary people are beginning to be better off. Overall a democratic, albeit often corrupt system of government is firmly in place, less unstable than before, though intrigues continue and coups are still not impossible. The Philippines adopts a consistently pro-Western stance in world politics and fulfils its obligations regionally by belonging to ASEAN, and the Asian Development Bank.

The other lands below the wind are increasingly prosperous and stable, some more than others. The racial strife and discrimination that used to plague them has largely disappeared. The various insurrections are also now largely forgotten. Apart from a few local disturbances, peace now reigns everywhere. The Huaqiao, after surviving discrimination and persecution are largely accepted by the people among whom they live. More and more they are sharing their wealth and expertise with the indigenous people. As with the tribute-bearing states to the north, they play a major role investing in the ancestral country. All look forward to an increasingly secure and prosperous future.

5
The Ancestral Country: Changing Fast

Practically all Huaqiao, however they may differ, and wherever they may be, still look to China, their ancestral land. An Overseas Chinese may only be able to speak his native dialect with difficulty, still less any Mandarin, and barely write a character; or he may have such a close affiliation going back 200 years or more with the country of his adoption as to be almost indistinguishable from the local population. Or he may be fluent in Mandarin, well versed in Chinese literature, an avid reader of the Chinese press, active in local clan affairs, an investor in the motherland with distant relatives still living in the native village in Guangdong, or Fujian, or Hainan. For all there is a certain bond that ties, a sense of so called Chineseness, whereby Chinese stick together, help each other, feel different to the rest. This of course will not stop them quarrelling with each other, even fighting or having totally different strongly held views. Nor does it obviate regional feelings, where Chinese from one province are wary of those from another and make rude remarks about their language and habits. These are the people who still, in the vernacular, often call themselves 'sons and daughters of the Yellow Emperor'. Origin and history are as relevant now as it was when their forbears first left home. To understand the Huaqiao you must appreciate their Chinese roots.

A mythical Emperor ruled over an area in the Yellow River basin, peopled by a few millions, some nomadic, some settled. The first dynasty, according to the traditional Chinese calendar, was the still rather shadowy Xia, 2205–1766 BC, followed by the Shang. Scholars generally accept this to be the starting point of recorded Chinese history, say nearly 4,000 years ago. By the time of the Zhou dynasty, about a millennium later, the written language had evolved and was reaching its present form, there was an organised hierarchical society and records of wars, successions, and disasters were being kept. The first ever was the Book of History, followed by the Book of Rites, which among other explained the concept of the Mandate of Heaven, whereby should an emperor rule badly he forfeits his right to do so, and should be replaced. This ancient dictum has provided the moral basis for Chinese to get rid of bad rulers ever since, not that it has always been applied. Other records narrated the histories of the kingdoms and their rulers and governments, their noble statesmen and brave generals. In time one kingdom grew stronger than the rest, defeated its rivals north, south and west, fended off barbarian tribes, spreading Chinese rule. This was the Qin, whose ferocious ruler could be called the first of a long line of Emperors to rule all China. The common people were almost entirely peasants tilling the soil, some bonded, some free: there were a few craftsmen and artisans. Most lived in small villages, some in towns, all were liable to military service on the rulers orders.

By about 500 BC there arose a group of men who propounded several social and moral codes that ordered society and influenced relationships right up to the collapse of the empire in 1912. Indeed, they influence Chinese thinking to this day. Of these, the most famous was Confucius (the Latinised version of his name given by the Jesuits). His thinking introduced moral concepts by which one should lead one's life. For example, functions should correspond to the names given them, so the ruler should rule, the minister be minister, the father, father and so on. In society everyone should do what he ought to do: there was a concept of duty, thus 'do not do to others what you do not wish for yourself'. So one should not act for profit, one should act to fulfil responsibilities. This concept of duty and the common good came to imbue the ruling classes of China; the idea that the community's welfare was more important than that of the individual is still strongly held today. What later became known as the Confucian Canon included the Five Classics: the mystical *Book of Changes*, the *Book of History*, the *Book of Rites*, the *Book of Odes*, the *Spring and Autumn Annals*, all of which predated Confucius; also the *Analects* of Confucius, a record of the Master's sayings, the *Mencius*, the *Great Learning*, the *Doctrine of the Mean*, constituted the Four Books. Some of these were edited by Confucius, some quote him and parts were nothing to do with him at all. All Confucian sayings and thoughts were venerated and their content became an obligatory part of all formal education. This was practised by all educated Chinese both in China and overseas until the end of the empire, subsequently by most until relatively modern times. Confucian thinking is to be found to this day, having survived nationalism, communism, technology and politics.

Confucius' disciple, Mencius, represented the more idealistic side of Confucian thinking, saying that man is by nature good, and everyone possesses an intrinsic compassion, or benevolence, for others. So good rulers ruled with moral instruction, bad rulers through force. He also considered ability more important than heredity in choosing a ruler; that hungry people cannot be relied upon to be moral. Perhaps Mencius' thinking may be best defined by the saying that virtue, that is goodness, brings success. Two other equally weighty, but less famous philosophers of the time were Modi and Xunzi. The former was an individualist who did not accept the established order, as did his peers. The latter, Xunzi, the fourth great figure among the Zhou philosophers believed human nature to be intrinsically bad: 'the nature of man is evil, his goodness is acquired training'. A little later, around 200 BC at a time when the Qin emperor was leading his armies against surrounding states, soon to win and establish what was the first dynasty to rule China, the Legalists began to teach a theory on method of governance that was totalitarian. The most famous, Han Feizi, considered it was not enough to appeal to the past to justify the present, but that new problems called for new measures. In order to ensure that nothing would be done incorrectly stringent attention to one's duties was called for. Savage retribution would be meted out to those who failed. All these thinkers and their writings were studied in most Overseas Chinese settlements just as much as in China.

The second great philosophy of the time was quite different. The starting point of Taoist (Daoist) philosophy is the preservation of life and the avoidance of injury. This included a negative escapism and an understanding of the basic laws of the universe; the needs of society, duties and responsibilities, were not included. The Dao De Jing, attributed to Laotse, who lived about 500 BC, stated that Tao (Dao) the way, lay hidden and was nameless. So 'do nothing, and there is nothing that is not done. Do not acknowledge a problem and it will go away'. This slightly fey reasoning appealed to many Chinese of the time, with its attendant mystery and magic. It also included the concept of *yin*, female, dark, *yang*, male, bright as basic elements of the cosmos. Taoism became an established religion with temples and monks, and continues to this day. As Confucianism represented authority so Taoism suited a more individual approach and in a corrupted form it provided the ethos of the secret societies set up in the 17th century with the aim of restoring the recently deposed Ming. These later degenerated into criminal associations and they still flourish in Hong Kong and South-East Asia, to revive in recent years in the southeast of China. Chinese martial arts are largely Taoist, as is demonology, much folklore and fairy tales of magic and mystery.

By the time of the beginning of the Han, China's first great dynasty, after whom the Chinese race is still named, an enduring pattern of society and government began to form and emerge. It was based on the largely Confucian thinking just described, and formed the basis of most social and political thinking for nearly 2,000 years. It was also roughly at about this time that the first settlers left the Guangdong and Fujian coasts for the unknown waters of Nanyang. In those days peasants, some still bonded, more of them free than before, worked the land all over China and looked to the squire, a member of what came to be called the scholar gentry, for leadership and support. These gentry were mostly literate, numerate, versed in the classics, conscious of duties and responsibilities to those above and those below them. They reported hierarchically to the provincial viceroy and he in turn to the Son of Heaven, the Emperor. Their sons, never their daughters, sat the imperial exams, based almost entirely on the Confucian Canon, to enter government service. In fact, these exams were in theory open to all ages, and there were recorded cases of old men of 70 turning up to have a go. The scholar gentry, imbued with this learning and this code, were not only responsible for administration, but also law and order, public works; in time of crisis officering the militia, in time of flood and famine organising relief. Such an enduring system inculcated a respect for learning that is still extremely strong in China. This tradition also exists among the Huaqiao: the teacher is a person to be respected, academic distinction is admired.

Meanwhile, China imported ideas from abroad for the first time ever. Some intrepid Indian Buddhist monks scaled the great mountains and found their way to the Han court; the Emperor was fascinated by what they had to say and sent his representatives to find out more. Buddhism soon became one of the three religions of China, as well as Taoism and Confucianism, although the latter was more a code of conduct than a faith. The main concept of the Confucian canon is that the life of a being is only one aspect in the cycle of cause and effect and death is not the end. What a person is now is an aspect of past life, what he does now will determine his future life, that is life after death. Such a tolerant and flexible creed remains popular to this day. Chinese communities both inside and outside the ancestral country have access to priests and temples (the harsh proscriptions of Communist rulers are long since gone). Many Chinese, particularly Overseas Chinese and Hong Kong businessmen, have a practical and flexible view on such matters; some wealthy Chinese may even hedge their bets and have both Buddhist and Taoist priests attend their funerals. Buddhism with its doctrines of karma, reincarnation and compassion has had a most profound effect on Chinese society, as much as any other idea imported from abroad. Other examples are far more recent: communism, which only lasted for less than a couple of generations from Liberation in 1949 to 1978 with the advent of the Open Door, before starting to transform itself into a form of capitalism with a strong thread of socialism. All these creeds and thoughts, including also additions such as Christianity, socialism, democracy, are to be viewed against a basic nationalism, pride of race and consciousness of Han supremacy. These ideas are also to be found in Nanyang where evidence of Chinese beliefs may be encountered all over the region. There are Confucian, Taoist and Buddhist temples, principally the latter, to be found in every township or district where Chinese have settled in any number. All have priests to cope with the numerous worshippers and accept alms. Some temples date back many hundreds of years, some are comparatively new.

This was the system that ruled China. The empire became larger as it pushed back the barbarian tribes and sinicised the southern provinces such as Guangdong, richer and stronger as the economy grew and crop yield increased, merchants travelled the well policed highways, sailed up and down the coast in huge junks, later to venture further afield. The Tang dynasty (AD618–906) saw China reach the zenith of her power, to be judged in the light of history as intellectually and physically the most powerful nation on earth at that time, yet still knowing practically nothing about the lands that lay to the west, and they of China. This was also a period of great artistic achievement, poetry and literature. To this day the Cantonese call themselves the men of Tong (Tang). Then followed the weaker, yet equally prominent intellectually Song, famous for its poets, thinkers and artists, to be driven south of the Yangzi by the invading Mongols of Genghis Khan who called themselves the Yuan dynasty; their horsemen conquered all Asia, reaching even as far south as Nanyang and as far west as Eastern Europe. After overrunning China, and causing massive destruction, the Mongols lost their hold and were followed by a native Chinese dynasty, the Ming, who formally began their reign in 1368. Despite the recent wars, society and economy recovered fairly quickly; there was growth, population increased to some 200 million, agricultural production increased. Communications improved considerably with the building of the Grand Canal linking north and south, plus a network of smaller canals across the country. There were simple banks, paper money, and movable type for printing long before its invention in Europe; pre-modern industry grew with the mining of coal, the smelting of iron, the firing of porcelain. There were explosives, paddle-wheel ships, junks navigated by magnetic compass, a rudimentary postal service and a huge standing army of three million men. Logistically, administratively, organisationally Ming China was a great and a powerful empire.

But around the year 1300 or so, a certain malaise had begun to influence Chinese thinking. The inventiveness and desire to seek new ideas had diminished, though technical invention continued. There was instead more of an adherence to the rules of the established order and little thought as to how to improve them. Chinese and Western scholars have debated the reasons for this without any definite conclusion. One theory is that everything was going so well there was really no point in seeking new ideas or new methods. Of course this had no perceptible impact then, or indeed for several hundred years, but it marked the beginning of a certain stagnation of Chinese thought that much later on, by the 19th century, resulted in an almost total unwillingness to accept anything new on the part of those in power and authority plus a state of what has been called wilful ignorance on the part of China's rulers. It could be this loss of impetus that resulted in a basic rigidity of thought and society, or that the dearth of any inventive thinking in the first place was the cause, or perhaps it was the lack of any new ideas entering China. Whatever the reasons for this stagnation of thought, it did China much harm, and contributed substantially to her later defeat at the hands of the West. Certainly Chinese thinking by this time often had difficulty in accepting new concepts. As an example, the discovery of another planet in the firmament was denied as the prescribed number of heavenly bodies had already been fulfilled. The geography of the lands beyond China was largely according to preconceived ideas; even that of South-East Asia was wildly inaccurate; Portugal for example was believed to be somewhere south of Java. The inward looking uninformed thinking of the time is further illustrated by the fact that when in 1842 the Court reluctantly agreed to cede Hong Kong to the British it took a long time to find it on the map.

The end of every dynasty was usually heralded by weak emperors, baleful intrigues at court, scheming eunuchs and indecisive leadership.

During the Song it was the Mongols who seized the chance in 1280; this time it was the Manchus in 1644. From their base beyond the pass leading down to the far northeast, their horsemen rode south and, with considerable help from dissenting Chinese generals, within a few years conquered all China. This was an alien rule, ably applied. The conquerors were nomads from the steppe, spoke no Chinese, worshipped different gods, and knew little of settled agriculture or town life. The conquering bannermen, as they were called, after the banners they carried into battle, were based in all the great cities and at strategic points throughout the empire. Local Chinese were also deployed in these garrisons and a system of dual command, Chinese and Manchu, developed throughout not only the military but the civil administration as well. With the capital now at Peking the new rulers set to work to consolidate their hold on China and beat off any opposition on the borders. So under Manchu rule, China conquered Tibet, what is now Xinjiang (Chinese Turkestan), extended Chinese rule into the border areas of Siberian Russia. In time, the tiny Manchu minority learned the language, and followed the customs with the exception of the Chinese foot binding of female children of the upper class. Meanwhile there had already been a few visitors from overseas, Arab traders who were allowed to set up a base at Zaiton in Fujian, one or two Dutch, English and Portuguese bold sea captains, and a group of intrepid Italian Jesuit priests including Matteo Ricci who were allowed to live in Peking and even attempted to convert officials to Christianity. The most noteworthy mission occurred later, at the end of the 18th century, when a British delegation sent by King George III of England to open up trading relations was told by the Emperor Qian Long that the Empire had all things in abundance and no need of any foreign goods at all. By this time the British, well established in India, were successfully seeking a foothold in South-East Asia, the Dutch were long established in Indonesia, the Spanish in the Philippines.

Other missions at about this time were equally unsuccessful. It was by then well known that China did not accept that any other nation could trade with her on equal terms; all the Chinese could accept was they be classified as barbarians bearing tribute and treated accordingly. In 1841 the British then forced their way into China with the first Opium War, marching north, forcing the Chinese to admit foreign trade. A roughly similar exercise happened in 1860 when a combined British and French force occupied the capital, burnt the Summer Palace and exacted a heavy indemnity. Meanwhile, a huge peasant rebellion, the Taiping, devastated much of central China, only to be put down with difficulty. Some of the fleeing rebels found their way to Nanyang, either overland or by sea, forerunners of a greater influx to come. Further humiliation followed as the century progressed and it was a surprise to many that China somehow seemed to survive as an independent state, unlike India and all the other colonial territories being rapidly established in Asia and Africa. However, by the end of the century China's foreign trade, banking system, early industry, even her customs service, was controlled by the West. Along the coast, up the great rivers, at all strategic points were so called Treaty Ports, territory where the Chinese writ did not run and the foreigner lived in a safe haven for his business and his residence, with his own garrison, police, and civil administration. Meanwhile, the Russians encroached on Chinese territory along the Siberian border, the Japanese took over the vassal state of Korea and annexed Taiwan, the British extended their rule over Hong Kong, the French occupied Kwangchouwan near their Indo-China colony, the Germans took Qingdao, and so on. It was called 'cutting up the Chinese melon'. Another saying, also coined by journalists, and in vogue at the time was that 'the affairs of China are settled in Europe'. China was, to a large degree, in semi-colonial status with all the drawbacks and none of the advantages such as military protection and law and order. It was also by then being used as a recruiting ground supplying cheap labour to the new rubber plantations in South-East Asia.

A few determined Chinese statesmen made a brave attempt to save the Empire in the 1870s, aptly called the last stand of Chinese conservatism. But it was to no avail; a weak emperor was dominated by the unscrupulous Empress Dowager, intent on power and patronage with no true understanding of the threat to China and the issues at stake, and there was no support from the court for any attempt at reform. While all this was going on the great mass of peasantry carried on living as they had done for hundreds of years, however the administration was becoming venal and the security and support from the scholar gentry was eroding. An anti-foreign nationalistic outburst, the Boxer rebellion, was crushed by allied arms in 1900 with considerable loss of life and the occupation of much of north China, including the capital. Humiliation seemed complete as yet another huge indemnity was imposed and once again the Court fled. All this had to end and after several attempts the revolutionary party the Tungmenghui toppled the Manchu dynasty with surprising ease and proclaimed the Republic of China in January 1912. Over 2,000 years of imperial rule was over. The Overseas Chinese of South-East Asia greeted the new government with enthusiasm. The West, for the most part, wished the new rulers well and that was all. There were of course well meaning missionaries and a few eccentric foreigners who cared for China. But the bulk of the Western resident population was in business and had no other aim but to make money. Their attitude was often one of amused contempt for what they sometimes called 'John Chinaman', a term first used by sailors off ships calling at Canton in the late 18th century as they roistered in the stews of Hog Lane near the docks, outside the city walls.

The overwhelming majority of the population carried on exactly as before, tilling the soil, rice in the south, maize in the north, catching fish, weaving cloth, organised into clans and guilds. But the backup of the old system had gone, and hard times, exacerbated by bandits or freebooting warlords, became more and more common. Westernisation had only affected a few cities, in particular Shanghai, to a much lesser extent Tianjin, Qingdao, Canton, along the coast. The Treaty Ports went merrily on; foreigners and many Chinese sheltered in them as rival warlord armies marched up and down the country. The leaders of the new Republic of China, led by Dr Sun Yat-sen as President did their best, but they were hamstrung; all north China was under control of a military clique headed by Marshal Yuan Shi-kai, warlord, intriguer, politician. However, China did make a start to try and assert her international rights, receiving sympathy if little else from most, but tangible assistance from the United States. China declared war against Germany on the side of the Allies in 1916 in the hope of some later support against Japanese encroachment. At the Versailles Treaty this was ignored as Japan pressed her infamous 21 Demands, which would limit China's economic independence and turn her into a near colony. For the first time in Chinese history the people showed their will. Thousands of students in Peking demonstrated on 4 May 1919, a day recorded in history, and made their point. This was a turning point in history and the 'five four' movement is regularly quoted to this day. These events were closely followed in Nanyang, whose Overseas Chinese population supported the struggling new Republic of China with plans for increased trade and investment, more contact and visits home.

After Dr Sun's death in 1925, the new President, later also Generalissimo, Chiang Kai-shek, soldier, patriot and autocrat organised an expedition from the Republic's southern base at Canton to march north and unify the country. By 1928, Chiang had defeated or won over warlords in north China, strangled the nascent Communist forces in Shanghai (an ally at that time) and more or less united China. It seemed the new regime might have a chance after all. A brief golden era, only a few years, ensued in the arts and literature, new ideas from outside were debated and innovative thought flourished. The new government established active consulates throughout Nanyang which became a focal point for a new found Chinese patriotism. Some of the powers handed their Treaty Ports back, the economy improved, peace was more or less established. But this was only a brief respite. In 1937 Japan, having already occupied Manchukuo (Manchuria) and after years of intermittent hostility launched an all-out attack on China as part of a grandiose scheme to dominate East Asia. Meanwhile, the foreigners continued to control the banks, the ports, the manufacture, and the trade. Some Chinese were able to move in as well, but not many. A few years before the Communist Party had formed a base at Jingangshan under its later to be world famous leaders, Mao Zedong, Zhou Enlai, Zhu De. A succession of encirclements by superior Nationalist forces obliged them to break out and, in 1934–5 the famous Long March took place. Some 20,000 Communist soldiers survived a year long, 10,000 li (3,000 miles) march from Southeast China across difficult and hostile terrain to finally end up in Yanan, in remote Shaanxi province in the north west. From here they lived to fight another day, finally to win all China.

During World War II, over 20 million Chinese died. Most industry was destroyed, the country ravaged, cities bombed flat. Japanese troops committed appalling atrocities including the so-called rape of Nanjing, the capital, with wholesale slaughter of civilians. At one stage they occupied over half the country and encouraged the smoking of opium to debase the people still further. China fought bravely but by war end the Nationalist forces were largely exhausted and demoralised. Corruption was rife at all levels. The Communist minority meanwhile had grown greatly in strength and size of area controlled. Post-war talks aimed at a settlement, chaired by the Americans, were a failure and in 1946 civil war resumed. Once more the civilian population suffered as great battles took place, ending in a total Nationalist defeat and withdrawal to Taiwan. In Peking on 1 October 1949, Mao Zedong proclaimed the Peoples Republic of China, saying that the Chinese people had stood up. Nobody knew what would happen next. Mao had already said that China would 'lean to one side'; it was firmly in the Soviet camp and the Cold War was at its height. Quite suddenly, for the first time ever, people were a little afraid of China. No one on the outside knew what was going on and it was just about impossible to find out. The only information forthcoming from the Chinese authorities were strident announcements of increased production and social progress, interspersed with praise for the Communist Party and its great leader. Most of the Overseas Chinese decided to wait and see what happened. There was encouragement by the People's Republic of Communist rebellions in Malaya and the Philippines, encouragement and material assistance in Vietnam: these and other similar actions seriously affected relations with Nanyang for many years. There were fears China might attempt a takeover of South-East Asia.

The new People's Government set to work with a will. There was a massive task of reconstruction after many years of war, both national and civil. Industry was destroyed, agriculture had been neglected, and people were starving. A new Communist order was introduced; a command economy, communal living on collective farms, in towns and in factories. Private ownership was abolished, this was a one-party state and the Communist Party ruled China. There was also a strong appeal to nationalism, many Chinese who disliked communism were nonetheless pleased and proud to see their country becoming strong again and treated with respect abroad. In rapid succession China got rid of all the landlords and capitalists, mostly by confiscation and purges. The people were mobilised to increase production, rebuild towns, start new industries. Tight fiscal control and the elimination of private banking rapidly reduced the runaway inflation. Public health improved, there was enough to eat, law and order prevailed. Life was not too bad as long as you accepted being part of the system. Any opposition was ruthlessly crushed; labour reform camps were established where inmates were brainwashed until they saw the light. China was a sealed country, and published no statistics. Her overseas trade at this time was minimal, only 2% of GDP. Everything, from thought to production to manufacture, was home grown. The only major act beyond her borders was to take part in the Korean War. This was a straight takeover bid by Communist North Korea against the South; opposed by the UN who sent troops, mostly American, but also British, Australian, Canadian, French and others. The war lasted three years and losses were heavy; some estimates put Chinese casualties at about a million.

China also made her position clear vis-à-vis the autonomous regions by invading Tibet and increasing control over the national minorities to the West. She also fought a short border war with India in 1962 and gave massive aid to Vietnam during the two wars. Elsewhere she raised the flag of revolution, exhorting all peoples, wherever they were, to rise up, cast out the imperialists and establish socialism, intervening where possible, particularly in South-East Asia. Her foreign relations were one-sided and difficult. At home the massive programme of reconstruction and communisation proceeded apace, results were good. For the first time there was a long period of peace and people felt secure, provided always they toed the party line. In 1958, the first catastrophic blunder came when Mao instigated the Great Leap Forward, a rapid attempt to increase production to catch up with the West. Millions were mobilised on impractical projects such as home-grown steel furnaces and agricultural production suffered greatly. The resultant famine laid waste to large tracts of countryside and approximately 30 million people died. Mao was then shunted sideways by the rest of the leadership, although still called Chairman and Great Helmsman. In 1965, he re-established his personal power by empowering the youth of the country to smash old traditions, including the Party. This was the Cultural Revolution – neither cultural nor a true revolution. It turned the country upside down, disrupted production, set education back a decade, destroyed communities and nearly ruined China. Mao died in 1976, not long after the Cultural Revolution was over and what was still called its gains were being evaluated. Following a brief interregnum and some tense political jockeying, Deng Xiaoping came to power and announced the Open Door Policy in 1978. These traumatic events greatly altered relations with Overseas Chinese. Under Mao they visited China seldom and could do little business if they did. Throughout the 1950s, 1960s and early 1970s relations were inhibited by Chinese intervention in the region. Under Deng they embarked upon a dramatic surge of business and contact which still shows no sign of lessening.

During the turbulent and unpredictable years of Mao's rule of China it seemed to the colonial rulers of South-East Asia, and their successors, also indeed much of the population that China had designs on all Nanyang. Throughout the Malayan Emergency, 1948–60, Radio Nanning in South China broadcast regularly in support of the Communist insurgents. There were rumours of Chinese arms reaching Malaya either by sea landing on remote stretches of coast, or over the border and through the jungle from Thailand. This was later found to be untrue, the distances and difficulties were too great: the only support the bandits got from China was verbal. Similarly, Chinese broadcasts were likewise beamed at the Philippines whose army was locked in battle with the Hukbalahap rebels at the same time. However, Chinese aid was well known to be much more than talk when it came to the wars in Vietnam; Mao himself later told a visiting French delegation in 1964 how his men had beaten their compatriots in battle a decade before. Such intervention was made possible by the long and porous frontier between the two countries. China has an even longer frontier with Burma and for a long time also announced unequivocal support for the Burma Communist Party though it never actively interfered as in Vietnam. The largest, and most vulnerable of the Nanyang countries was Indonesia, by the early 1960s close to economic collapse and riven by factions. A well prepared coup d'etat in 1965 was countered by a successful right-wing coup by generals. There were tales, never conclusively proved, that the first coup was backed by clandestine arms shipments from China. During all these years, Communist China, often called the Reds, or the Chicoms, was seen as a major threat to regional security. In some instances, the threat was countered locally as in Malaya, in some it succeeded as in Vietnam, to be subsumed into independent nationalism. In Indonesia it resulted in a military controlled government that took over and ran the country for a generation until it foundered in its own incompetence. As the countries of South-East Asia became stronger and more stable, so the threat was turned. Most important, China herself, after the excesses of the 1950s, the turmoil of the Cultural Revolution in the 1960s, calmed down, heralding a more undecided 1970s which culminated in the greatest change of all. The threat to Nanyang ceased to exist with the Open Door.

What then followed set in train an irreversible process. Foreign businesses were allowed to invest in China, either alone, or with Chinese partners. For the first time in 30 years China was open to the world. Outside capital was welcome, foreign businesses could contact their Chinese opposites direct, rather than through the state. The massive command economy system was in part dismantled. Growth was stimulated by new freedoms. The dormant Chinese entrepreneurial spirit was re-awakened. There were several types of participation permitted, the actual input of capital and technology, manufacture under license, collaboration by contract and the so-called 'buy back' system. The investor would ship plant or machinery into China, which immediately became the property of the Chinese partner who would commence production right away. The investor would then 'buy back' the production at a specially low rate over a fixed period, say five years. A large proportion of Hong Kong and Overseas Chinese investment is of this type. The difficulties for foreign investors were however considerable; it was hard to find the right Chinese partner and really no way of verifying if the correct choice had been made. The Chinese were totally unused to Western or outside business methods, and vice versa. Regulations were at times unclear, subject to frequent change and could be differently interpreted. Usually the Western side would put in capital, equipment, technology and management; the Chinese would contribute the site, the buildings, some management, the labour. Overseas sales were usually handled by the foreigner, internal by the Chinese.

Misunderstandings and disappointments were legion. In time, things got better and within a decade or more it was estimated that about 20% of Chinese industry had a foreign element. All these developments were followed with great interest by Huaqiao everywhere who were among the first to get involved. The wars and rebellions were forgotten. The numbers visiting the ancestral country rocketed.

The authorities also created a series of Special Economic Zones and other zones where restrictions on manufacture and commercial activity were largely lifted, to encourage economic activity. Many of these were on the sites once occupied by the old Treaty Ports, centres of economic activity and communication. The most famous, and most successful was in the south, the Shenzhen Zone, where a small town rapidly became a hive of manufacturing and commercial activity with a population that quickly grew tenfold. Meanwhile the shackles on agricultural production were lifted by the responsibility system. Hitherto, the peasantry grouped into communes, had a norm to fulfill and that was that. Now, they still had a set target, but anything over and above they could keep. Production soared, and helped finance the massive industrial growth that began to pervade the country. A similar responsibility system for industry was also introduced but not so successfully at first. More economic autonomy was given to provincial authorities to make decisions, approve projects, allocate resources. Sometimes rules would be bent to achieve more freedom from central control. Meanwhile, information began to become readily available, albeit often inaccurate, and questions were now sometimes being answered. This was still a country where no industrial or trade directories were available; such information was usually gleaned and collated by the outside agencies in the West and elsewhere who were promoting trade with China.

All these great changes brought about the return of one of China's traditional ills: official corruption. At the same time, the command economy system that was imposed on China in 1950 was increasingly by-passed. Hitherto all outside businesses, buying from a foreign manufacturer, selling to a foreign importer, could only be conducted via one of the Foreign Trading Corporations. There were eight of these, headquartered in Peking, with branches in all the major cities. Everything, and anything, went through this slow bottleneck, a system that was honest but only worked well with small volumes of business. The seller practically never met the buyer and vice versa. Now it was different. Direct contact increased. The old remained but was increasingly side-tracked. Greater numbers of foreign businessmen visited Chinese factories for direct dealing, increasing numbers of Chinese missions travelled abroad. The twice annual Canton Export Commodities Fair still continued but no longer was the focus of all overseas sales. All these changes made for great confusion. Slowly, it became easier. Numerous consultants, both Western and Chinese jumped on the bandwagon of explaining and interpreting what was now going on; many were spurious and quickly discredited. Seminars on how to do business in China were held all over the Western world. Numerous books on the subject began to appear, of very varying standard. Practically all were written by foreigners.

There was also legal reform, with a new, fairly comprehensive code promulgated in 1982. For the first time in 30 years Chinese lawyers were allowed to set up practice. The rules of accountancy were revised. There was a new taxation system and it gradually became possible to understand this hitherto arcane subject. More and more Western firms, many with Hong Kong affiliations, moved into Peking and other major cities. The commercial offices of the foreign embassies in China went into overdrive; Chinese embassies abroad were forthcoming and far more informative. It became easier for the business visitor to China to get a visa; no longer the frustrating wait. Travel round China became simpler, more Western-style hotels became available. Foreign visitors could now choose where to stay, and make their own travel arrangements as well. Meanwhile numerous Chinese private enterprises, to buy, to sell, to do both, were set up. Many, if not most, did not go through the usual capital formation process. They were often already in situ, hived off from a municipal or provincial government body. So the head of a local government department in a large provincial city would at the same time be president of a private enterprise that engaged in parallel activities. His official visiting card and his private business visiting card could well give the same address and telephone numbers. The 1980s were a time of great growth and great confusion. There were also changes to the infrastructure with more high-rise buildings beginning to appear in provincial towns and a great increase in the study of English.

The China of today is already an economic giant. Recent remarkable growth in the Chinese manufacturing industries has led to a steady surge in exports, particularly to Europe and the US and has caused dispute and complaint; cheap Chinese goods such as clothes, footwear, toys have flooded the shops; the United States already has a massive and growing balance of payments problem with China. This problem is exacerbated by the pegging of the Chinese yuan to the American dollar some years ago; this has been slightly modified and the debate now is whether this can be completely changed, or a floating rate introduced. Nowadays, throughout the West, not only is the 'Made in China' label to be seen in every shop, there are increasing numbers of Chinese tourists in the street, and thousands of young Chinese students at every university (some 60,000 in the UK alone). Fortunately, these and other possible causes of tension are being tackled on the Chinese side by a leadership which, while doing its best to further Chinese interests, will not push matters so far as to provoke irrevocable antagonism and hostility on the world markets. After all, it should be remembered that the Three Represents, enunciated by Jiang Zemin after the 16th Communist Party Congress in 2002 were very clear. These laid down the following aims: the interests of the Chinese economy, the development of Chinese culture, the needs of the Chinese people. This is a government that knows what it wants and how far it can go, that is directing the transition of the economy into a form of market capitalism part still state-owned, a process now well advanced. Certain principles, including some of those that guided the leadership over 50 years ago, while no doubt adjusted to fit the modern situation, continue to apply. Mao's portrait is still there for the entire world to see at Tiananmen, despite all the recent obloquy.

About two-thirds of the huge workforce, less than before, is on the land. Agricultural production is still just enough to feed the population and create some surplus although grain is bought from abroad. Population growth continues but is slowing, and is estimated to peak half way through the century. The draconian measures such as one child per couple have had their effect, a reduction of population growth on one hand, spoilt, obese middle class children on the other, and an increase in bachelors. There has also been an increase in female infanticide in poor rural areas. The infrastructure, road, rail, water transport copes though frequently overloaded, and bottlenecks are common; however the days when one province starved while the next one had plenty are long gone. Nevertheless the pressure is intense and shows no signs of abating. A vast programme of highway expansion is under way; there is a total of a million kilometres of roads (a tenfold increase since 1949), now including 11,000 km of expressway. Along these roads run lorries, also increasingly private cars. About two million cars a year are manufactured, by numerous enterprises, some of them joint ventures with well known Western makers. Sales are huge, and growing. The resultant need for oil has far outstripped China's domestic production; imports from the Middle East are growing and forcing up international petroleum prices. The pollution is appalling, particularly in great cities with dense layers of smog. These problems are recognised and being tackled: with attempts, not all successful, to control rigorous carbon dioxide emissions and the like. To date it has little effect; likewise attempts to limit car ownership are not successful. Driving standards are low, there are jams, delays and frequent horrendous accidents. The railways are barely adequate and now subject to constant delays. The growth of the infrastructure can barely keep up with the growth of the economy. Problems are exacerbated by frequent electricity and water shortages. China is stretched to the limit.

As in 19th-century Europe, the growth of industry has caused a shift from countryside to town, and all major cities have large bodies of itinerant workers looking for jobs. The huge industrial sector is growing with little sign of slowing down. China relies on coal, about 2,000 million tons a year are dug, providing about three-quarters of all China's energy needs. There are reports of poor safety measures in some of the mines and consequent terrible accidents. Steel production is also huge, at 250 million tons a year. Most of the heavy industry, and all of the defence industry, supporting nearly three million men under arms, are still under state ownership and certain to remain so; steps are being taken to modernise and improve management. Throughout China there is much exploitation, pay is poor, regulations are often broken, hours are long, accommodation often minimal if not wretched. The old days of the 'iron rice bowl' whereby workers in a factory received a pittance in wages, but prices were very low and they received near free accommodation, schooling for children, medical attention, all part of the deal, have largely gone. Other industries, such as shipbuilding, vehicle manufacture, petrochemical, building materials, iron smelting, fertiliser, pottery are sited in the traditional industrial areas of the north east, and along the eastern seaboard, once surprisingly poetically described at the beginning of industrialisation early in the 20th century, as the modern fringe stitched along 'the hem on an ancient garment (*China Proper*, a handbook prepared by the Intelligence Division, Royal Navy). Light industry, plastics, textiles, electronics instruments etc. are to be found all over China, policy is to encourage growth in the less developed western part of the country.

The general statistics continue to be arresting. Exports have more than doubled since China joined the World Trade Organisation at the end of 2001 and now have reached a yearly total of about US$600 billion, consisting chiefly of clothing, textiles, toys, furniture, electrical machinery, chemicals, electronics; imports at about US$540 billion principally consist of advanced technology, precision instruments, vehicles, machinery, metals, grain, oil; the balance of trade is in China's favour. Over 40% of the GDP is attributable to industry, while about a third is rural. In 2003, total inward foreign investment was around US$50 billion (of which half came from Hong Kong and South-East Asia). The total value of all investment in China is now at the staggering figure of US$500 billion. It must also be remembered that about 400 million people have been lifted out of poverty in the past 25 years. Public health is better, life expectancy longer. GDP per capita is now just over US$1,000 a year and despite some great failings, most people are far better off than ever before. Human rights abuses continue as before and justice is hard to obtain for poor people. One difference is that such conditions are now widely known outside China. Another is that there are a number of brave lawyers who seek justice for ordinary people who have been abused by the system.

This is not the only change; the Internet is in common use, as are mobile phones, particularly in the cities where ownership of a TV and a refrigerator is now the rule, rather than the exception. Indeed, there is a great gap between prosperous middle-class Chinese living in the great cities and the still very poor peasantry or itinerant industrial workers. Despite periodic clampdowns and censorship, with no prospect of a plural democracy in sight, the people have access to information in a way they never did before. All sorts of issues are discussed that never reach the newspapers, though this too is just beginning to change. Items are now reported in the national and provincial press such as safety scandals, industrial accidents, and official incompetence. In fact the biggest danger to Chinese society now chiefly lies in a possible widening of the gap between rich and poor.

6
Talking Business: Towkays, Tjukongs and Kongsis

The above terms mean, in order, boss, supporter, company. All are based on original Chinese dialect terms and have been part of the South-East Asian language scene for hundreds of years. They are in common use throughout Nanyang where as is well known, business methods differ considerably from those in China. But certain basic traits and attitudes are roughly similar, the product of a common heritage. Huaqiao businessmen usually enjoy a considerable advantage when dealing with their fellow South-East Asians. They are almost always better organised for business, have greater resources, can borrow more readily, exert influence with officialdom, and are able to call on a network of friends and contacts as required. They are not necessarily inscrutable as some Europeans who describe them would have it; few Chinese are. They are just usually more low key and outwardly less emotional when negotiating business; there are of course notable exceptions to this. All these factors have contrived frequently to place them in a position of advantage over most of their indigenous interlocutors. Their knowledge of their own language and the languages of their host countries varies greatly. Often negotiations are conducted entirely in English, the commercial lingua franca of the region, or in the languages of Nanyang, or in their dialects, also now increasingly in Mandarin. They are noted for being reliable and keeping promises; the term 'word of a Chinaman' originated in the region in the early 19th century among the early European colonials.

Mainland Chinese negotiating styles are changing as modernisation proceeds apace. But certain fundamental characteristics remain. Lateral communication is often slow and complex, contact is made through channels, up to the top, across, and so down again. This cumbersome procedure is still very common, though increasingly bypassed. It is now possible to settle a matter by a quick phone call to a *guanxi*, often translated as 'contact'. *Guanxi* is the basis of nearly all relationships, a guanxi oils the wheels, opens the door, smoothes the path. From time to time the Chinese side will withdraw to confer, or consult the leadership whether official body or now increasingly, private firm. A great cultural divide with the West is still apparent, with differing codes of values and ethics. The Confucian model of a hierarchical, ordered society where everyone, until the recent great changes, had his place and responsibilities is pitted against modern liberal capitalism, about which the Chinese themselves are learning fast. In this context they also often quote the saying whereby you 'take from the past what is good and leave what is bad'. This catch-all phrase covers just about everything, including much of China's recent history when things went so badly wrong and cannot easily be explained away.

There are certain definite negotiating styles. They will never push an opponent into a corner with no way out; they will always leave a ladder by which he may gracefully descend. Previously they were sometimes secretive, are now much less so. Certainly they are unwilling to admit any weakness or failing and thus lose face. They regard generous gestures usually with caution and cynicism. Why are they doing this? What is in it for them? They can be ruthless. Some foreign partners in joint ventures can be regarded as little better than a resource. They are capable of asking for all sorts of favours, and making unreasonable requests. Send us all your samples by air tomorrow. Come back for further talks next week, and so on. Speech is oblique, 'maybe' means no, to describe something by first saying 'it is very hard to say' means it is unspeakably awful. The Chinese attitude to the foreigner may be defined as one of cordial indifference. There is not too much attention to his views apart from the matter in hand; often plenty of material interest. How much do you earn? How much did your house cost? It might be summarised that the Chinese negotiate according to a set of rules they consider to be correct and fair, and which rules they reserve the right to alter, without notice, sometimes retrospectively. Like everything else on the Chinese business scene, this is changing.

The Huaqiao never had a rigid command economy imposed upon them, never went through the difficulties and restrictions of a People's Government. Nor indeed did they undergo the chaos and suffering visited upon China in recent years. Of course they too have suffered hardship, particularly in earlier days, also discrimination and difficulties, but of a totally different nature. So it may be concluded that some of the basic Chinese characteristics mentioned above are to be found in South-East Asia, but greatly altered. For a start, the Huaqiao left not only China but also the Chinese government. Their dealings with earlier colonial governments were mostly at one remove, those with the post-colonial independent governments sometimes greatly restricted, or they were abused, or mistreated, depending greatly on the territory. At no time were politics the stuff of their everyday life, at no time were they, willingly or unwillingly, part of a rigid system. So attitudes are more relaxed and the cultural gulf is not nearly so wide. Chinese and other races have lived together in South-East Asia for hundreds of years. There may be dislike, rivalry, envy, but seldom a failure of communication. The language problem is far less acute, misunderstandings far fewer. There is less formality, less rigid methodology. Overseas Chinese, unlike mainland Chinese, have not been so directly conditioned to fear and dislike the foreigner. They are still better informed about the outside world (though the mainlanders are catching up fast). Those in business are nearly all entrepreneurs of a sort, large or small. They do of course share a common ancestry whereby a hidebound government refused to accept dealings on equal terms with other nations until forced to do so. Unlike China, they do not present any apparent enigma to the outside world and have never been the subject of such intense speculation and analysis.

The Huaqiao business community, despite being, for the most part, modern, efficient, rapid and with huge resources is still largely organised along traditional lines. It shares certain fundamental traits with business in China; equally, some Overseas Chinese businesses are, apart from a little local colour, indistinguishable from comparable concerns in London, New York or Sydney. Some smaller and older firms still evoke romantic memories of Josef Conrad's stories of the region: the Kapitan China in upriver Borneo, the old *towkay* or merchant boss in Singapore's Chinatown, the *kongsi* or company in a *kampong* or village on the jungle edge, the master of a trading junk with lateen sails off the coast of Molucca, perhaps with the owner, a wealthy *tjukong* (business backer) and his client on board. Marked characteristics of course encompass *guanxi*, sometimes also rather woodenly translated as reciprocity, or even worse as interpersonal relationships. There is also *xinyong*, trust in each other, *mianzi* the concept of face or appearances, *ganqing* emotion, the ties that bind. Such feelings are not of course limited to Chinese only, others share them but perhaps not in such an intense and concentrated way. *Guanxi*, the most obvious and ubiquitous can be based on locality, dialect, having the same surname, being erstwhile classmates, or teacher and student, membership of the same society, co-worker in a firm, colleague in an office. A distinction should be made; *guanxi* is not the same as a trade or market exchange. It does not imply bribery and corruption though it can lead to it. It is of course, in common with many business practices, blatantly manipulative.

Since there was nothing to replace the Chinese government when they arrived in South-East Asia, the Chinese were far less constrained by bureaucracy. Indeed, they were usually debarred from becoming bureaucrats themselves by the colonial governments of the time, and it was virtually impossible for them to enter one of the professions. So in order to survive, the main aim, and to maintain self-esteem, the Huaqiao, as soon as they were in a position to do so, concentrated on trade and business. This was the obvious way forward and they used every possible social and political tie possible in order to succeed, choosing material progress via business as the yardstick of success, riches and wealth as the hallmark of ability and self-reliance. This success was sometimes manifested in ostentation and flagrant displays of wealth. The aim was also to ensure continuity. Rich Westernised Chinese merchant families sometimes sent their sons to English public schools or American colleges. Some young people excelled at leading British and American universities. They gave, generously but selectively, to charity partly through a Confucian sense of duty. They got to know the right people and cultivated them assiduously. In time they became an articulate and powerful minority, and like everyone else were aware of the social and political issues of the day in which they seldom directly intervened.

Chinese companies in South-East Asia tend to demonstrate certain management traits such as centralised decision-making, an emphasis on personal contact and tight control; loyalty is regarded as the most esteemed quality. A typical Nanyang company is, to this day, usually family-owned, with family members as directors, or if they are not bright enough, as privileged workers in easy positions. Usually a fairly small operation, there is a waged labour force, it is localised and deals with a particular commercial section of the economy such as import/export, or retailing. For these reasons the company usually belongs to a single ethnic or dialect group, yet there is generally plenty of internal competition. Should it grow into a large modern corporate enterprise, even a joint stock company, it will still be controlled and largely owned, by one family, or family grouping. Operating style is often imprecise, specifications are general, there are few specialised departments and individual duties vary greatly. The job description is a Western import. The leadership is mostly both authoritarian and secretive. It has been estimated by certain Western economic experts that such structures are good for three generations only before they disintegrate. In fact, names and composition can change over time while actual ownership remain unaltered. Indeed, the nature of Nanyang Chinese business does not lend itself to record keeping and analysis. There are many firms in the region that can point to far longer, albeit chequered, histories.

Confucianism is a source of attitudes and concepts. Despite all the great changes and upheavals over the past century, it is still apparent. There is, it is said, a cyclical view of time. There is forward planning but it is neither formal nor tabulated; another concept, that of the benchmark, is also a foreign addition. The social aspects of Confucianism have been enumerated and are readily apparent: the family, the hierarchy, the common good, the value of the institution, and duty to others, the cultural milieu. There is also a reverse side of the coin: nepotism, privilege, worry about how things appear, fear of being made to look inadequate in some way, the network of sometimes onerous obligations that have to be honoured, the non-objective assessment of performance. There is a hierarchical obligation, both lateral and vertical, that transcends all other relationships. A rich man's son passes his exams, becomes a bureaucrat or a professional, fulfils his duties and obligations to his family, employers, friends and of course himself. Duty has been done according to a Confucian code. Other Chinese traditional thinking, including Taoism, one of the three great religions of China, is apparent in abstract concept, myths and folklore. It impinges little on behaviour, both social and business. Buddhism is less a code of conduct or a concept of hierarchy, rather a belief in an enlightened afterlife. All the great Chinese religions can be adapted to a degree. Dogma is not rigid.

Practically all business of any sort, anywhere, at any level is conducted via *guanxi*, a personal network of friends and connections. Recommendations from these secure contracts and business entrees; there is often no need to look further. Sometimes international contacts come from relations abroad, an uncle and aunt in Toronto, a nephew or niece working in a London bank. This all-embracing networking ambience has over time also been grafted on to the indigenous elite of South-East Asia. Often the local aristocracy, Malay, Javanese, or Thai are brought into play to push a project. Probably they will have high-level connections in government, may well be related to a senior minister. It is generally accepted how the Malaysian

Government's bold and imaginative policy of favouring indigenous Malay business has been remarkably successful, both commercially and socially. It was readily backed by most of the Chinese who not only saw the good sense of such a measure, but also realised they themselves could benefit by new channels of access. It was also obvious that continued exclusion of the indigenous majority from business was in the long run going to be disastrous, such as the riots in Kuala Lumpur in 1969. So by working at all levels, up to local princelings, even sultans and rajahs, the Chinese *towkays* of Malaysia, the *tjukongs* of Indonesia with their *kongsis* have helped themselves. It is an enlightened form of self-interest.

So in Malaysia, the Chinese maintain their business ascendancy by allying themselves with local interests, at the same time strengthening overseas links for future expansion. Chinese businesses in Thailand are mostly in close cahoots with Thais, often of the elite or well connected. Many of these Thai Huaqiao are, as related, of mixed blood and assimilated to varying degrees into Thai society, speaking Thai as their first language, following Thai customs. In Indonesia the Chinese are distinct from the original inhabitants and have had a hard time of it as frequent objects of dislike and suspicion: they sometimes still do though persecution and discrimination are now fairly rare. Yet, despite all the many difficulties they have survived, and some have allied themselves with local interests to make great fortunes. As is general within the region it is a two-way trade. In the Philippines there has been, perhaps surprisingly due to the ethnic difference, considerable intermarriage and assimilation. In Burma, Vietnam, Laos, Cambodia there has been little difficulty and the Huaqiao have been largely assimilated, in these erstwhile tribute-bearing states. Yet there have been notable exceptions; Vietnam's harsh treatment of her Chinese minority was a principal cause of the Chinese military incursion of 1978. Throughout the whole region, the Chinese have adopted a low-key posture; chameleon like often adopting local names and customs, yet they are obviously different and Chinese efforts to conform are seldom completely successful.

An unsettling activity has been the secret societies throughout the region. Originally formed in South China over 300 years ago with the aim of overthrowing the Qing dynasty and restoring the Ming, these groups, some of which are known as Triads meaning: heaven, earth, water, have long since become criminal. They mostly arrived along with the 19th century immigrants into South-East Asia and are firmly entrenched throughout. They are extremely powerful and through blackmail, extortion and violence, control some specific aspects of commercial life, in particular the drug trade, gambling, prostitution, all sorts of vice and are responsible for much of the serious crime. Tightly knit, bound by oath, and closed to outsiders they frequently, in the course of gangland war, murder each other, and anyone else unwise enough to get in the way. Ordinary people are terrified of them. Linked by family ties, with contacts throughout the region including Hong Kong and now South China again, Triads and other societies also look to a spiritual and mystical basis for their actions, including ceremonies, incantation and special prayers. In most areas they have infiltrated both police and government.

With the exception of Singapore and Malaysia, government officials throughout Nanyang are frequently poorly paid, sometimes ludicrously so. It was estimated in Jakarta some years ago that the average government servant or army officer received a salary that would only keep him and his family for ten days in the month. In order to survive they had to, and still do, seek other work, or in many cases if there are opportunities, engage in petty corruption. So the policeman pardons the motorist and puts the discounted cash traffic fine in his pocket, the tax collector suggests a reduced bill and a commission, the planning official grants a permit on payment, factory inspectors turn a blind eye, customs officers help themselves to an open suitcase before waving it through. The sums are small, this is petty corruption, debasing and demoralising, deeply rooted and a seemingly ineradicable part of daily life. Chinese business people, active in commerce and industry, often wealthy, travelling frequently, are in constant need of official permission and pay readily. Some unfairly blame them on this source of corruption; they are not necessarily the instigators but are guilty of going along with a seemingly ineradicable system. Often of course a payment is not to obtain a favour or a privilege, it is merely to achieve receipt of something clearly approved and long overdue. A document at the bottom of a pile on an official's desk where it has lain for weeks, even months, will suddenly find its way to the top when matters have been arranged. In Chinese slang this is known as 'the goodness', in Indonesian, 'the morsel' or 'mouthful'. Such matters are in stark contrast to the large-scale bribery and corruption that regularly occurs at a high level in politics and business throughout much of the region. Presidents such as Suharto of Indonesia or Marcos of the Philippines had their price. Many of the protagonists are Chinese who usually do the paying, the locals the receiving. Throughout Nanyang corruption, to varying degree, pervades government and most official activity.

That it was difficult for Chinese to participate in Nanyang politics did not inhibit a minority of Huaqiao from participating in China politics: they joined Dr Sun and the Tungmenghui at the beginning of the 20th century, later Chiang Kai-shek and the Kuomintang, then Mao Zedong and the Communists. Previous internal regional politics have not attracted so much Chinese notice, with the formidable exception of the Communist insurrections. Not many Chinese fought for Sukarno and his men when they rose against the Dutch, nor supported Rizal in the Philippines when he rose against the Spaniards in 1898. They hardly ever took sides or joined political factions in Thailand and blended into the background. There is no political freedom in Burma anyway and the Huaqiao, as the army saying goes, mostly kept their heads down during the two great wars against France and against America in Vietnam. However, it is rather different in Malaysia where even during the Communist insurgency, the so-called Emergency, a system was evolving. Representing a third of the population and largely controlling the economy, the Malayan Chinese Association (MCA) came to form a powerful counterweight to the ruling UMNO (United Malay National Organisation). Over the years since independence in 1957, the Chinese have played an increasingly important political role through this vehicle. Both UMNO and the MCA form an alliance which, together with the Indian minority, makes Malaysia the success story of the region.

Since hardly any non-Chinese speak Chinese, most Huaqiao readily learn the language of their country of adoption, something they have done widely throughout South-East Asia, though in the back streets of Singapore you may perhaps still find a few old people who know only Hokkien, the dialect of Fujian province on the southeastern seaboard of China from where most Singaporeans originally came. The South-East Asian indigenous languages vary greatly; if from the former tribute bearing territories abutting China they are tonal and have some similarities in syntax, if further south, such as Malay or Tagalog, then are quite different in all respects. These southern languages have a high form, for example what used to be called Rajah Malay, spoken by the rulers and the nobility, with a more detailed grammatical structure, plus a simpler yet equally pure form spoken in the villages. Since Western colonisation became established, a bastardised common tongue also developed in the great cities and seaports, spoken by all races. In Singapore, Kuala Lumpur and other Malaysian cities, Bazaar Malay, as it is called, is a lingua franca with a vocabulary of only 500 or so words and is easy to pick up. Chinese businessmen, Indian shopkeepers,

European planters all learned it; the native Malays adjusted their speech accordingly. A similar situation also applies throughout the Indonesian archipelago; the original Rajah Malay has since been modified and modernised and is the medium for the press, government and any intellectual exchange; a refined version of Bahasa Kebangsaan, the language of the race. In recent years some languages have also taken on the names of their countries, thus Bahasa Malaysia, Bahasa Indonesia, Filipino. In the Philippines English is also spoken to a surprising degree in the villages. In Vietnam, Cambodia, Laos a few of the older bourgeoisie and upper class still speak French. Huaqiao speaking these local languages mostly have a distinctive accent and have difficulty with certain consonants, in particular the letter r pronounced as l, on occasion the subject of mimicry and derision by the local population.

There is one pre-eminent language, the most widely spoken by far in southern Nanyang: Indonesian, Bahasa Indonesia, the national language of over 200 million people (most of whom also have their own regional language), spoken also in a slightly different form as Malaysia's Bahasa Malaysia. If you speak it you can travel without let or hindrance from the Thai border, down through the Malayan peninsula to Singapore, across to Sumatra and so right through Indonesia from Sabang to Merauke. Bahasa Indonesia, Bahasa Malaysia, originally known as Malay is based on the language spoken by the inhabitants of Minangkabau, Sumatra long ago. It spread, and over time became a fairly standard form of communication, with considerable variations nonetheless, throughout Malaya, the Rhiau islands, Sumatra, the Borneo coast. On the more populous islands of Java and further east, Sulawesi, Maluku, Flores, other languages prevailed with some slight similarities but mutually unintelligible. The few who were literate, the scribes at court wrote in Sanskrit, for Hinduism was the prevailing religion of the time. Later, Indian and Arab traders brought Islam to the region and by about the year 1500 much of the region was converted. This meant the adoption of Arabic script which became, until recently, the principal method of writing Malay. It is an adapted script, for not all the Malay sound values match the Arabic, and is known as Jawi. Later, after 1945, when independence movements gathered force, language became a political issue. Citizens were urged to use their national language. There was also large-scale adaptation to Roman script for publishing in Malay/Bahasa Indonesia; newspapers, books, government literature, advertisements etc. though Arabic script remains in widespread use as a medium for religious instruction.

This is a deceptively easy language. As a well-known primer for learning Malay had it some 60 years ago: 'after three months you will think you know all there is to know, after three years you know you never will'. The basic structure is simple and you pronounce words as you read them. There are practically no grammatical rules, practically none of the paraphernalia surrounding Western languages. There are subtleties of inflection, word order, emphasis, that can tilt a meaning. You can get by on basic *kampong* (i.e. village) Malay provided you accept the limitation of the scope. For something more complex you build on the roots. Thus, as an example, 'satu' means one. Add a prefix and a suffix: 'persatuan': unity (a constant cry in Indonesia at Merdeka time). Or 'ada', there is, there are. 'keadaan': existence. 'Ingat', remember: 'ingatan', memory. Few other languages offer such a direct route from simple concept to abstract idea. It is not surprising the language spread; it is a language in which a conversation with a university professor or an illiterate peasant is equally possible. It lends itself to rhetoric, reportage and poetry. Bahasa Indonesia or Bahasa Malaysia is also a matter of national pride. For the indigenous it is their own language anyway, for the settlers be they Chinese, Indian or other, an easy vehicle for communication and now of course the official language. The main territory of southern Nanyang where Bahasa, as it is often called, is not spoken widely is the Philippines. Here it is Tagalog, the language of Luzon the northern island; spoken by about half the total population. There are some similarities to Malay. Just about all Filipinos also speak English and that is the true lingua franca of the country. The only major language of the region that no one ever learns is Chinese in any form.

Apart from some very long-established communities who have forgotten not only how to write but also how to speak Chinese, all Huaqiao have Chinese in various forms as their first language. It is one of the most ancient, difficult, complex yet efficient languages to exist. It largely ignores formal grammar and syntax, as for example in European languages, relying on word order and particles to indicate tense and order. It is written in a series of symbols or ideographs known as characters, each expressing a word and possessing an intrinsic monosyllabic pronunciation and tone, both of which vary widely according to which part of China the speaker is from. The simplest character consists of one stroke, the most complicated 48. There are about 7,000 to 8,000 in general use and it needs about 2,500 to read a newspaper; each has its own meaning and each one has to be learned individually. This written language is common to all Chinese wherever they may be;

it does not necessarily relate to the sound of what is said; there is little concordance between sound and symbol. It is therefore possible to learn to read and write Chinese without being able to speak a word. The spoken language varies widely but has a more or less common structure. The variety and flexibility of Chinese means there is nothing technical, scientific, philosophical, political, social that cannot be expressed. There is a great body of literature, ancient and modern; works written 2,500 years ago are still legible, albeit with difficulty.

A tone is the pitch or level at which a word is pronounced and is inherent. It is not the same as a sound which can be uttered in differing tones. Tones may rise, may fall, may do both, may be level; say one wrongly and it may represent something quite different and so another meaning. However in practise the meaning can be often guessed from the context. All characters have their intrinsic tone in which they must be pronounced when spoken; the wrong tone may result in the wrong character. A character is a written symbol that represents a one syllable word, for that is the basic structure of the language; however modern Chinese is mostly in a series of two or three characters strung together, each of these characters retains its own meaning, sound and tone. When linked with one or two other characters the compound so created has a different, but related meaning. Character writing can be an art in itself with calligraphers executing various styles by brush, though modern China writes mostly with a ballpoint pen. However penmanship is still esteemed, calligraphy is regarded as an art, and a good hand may excite comment. The actual writing of a character consists of executing strokes to a certain order and design which in each case have to be learned. Many characters are themselves made up from other characters. Like-sounding characters may sometimes look alike, similar characters may have similar meanings, though by no means always. There are no certain rules or guidelines for composing characters; it is however sometimes possible to guess the meaning by context or components. Above all there is no way you can spell Chinese, nor are there any shortcuts.

The very first written Chinese was essentially a picture language, with drawings depicting basic things such as fire, wood, sun, horse, cart, man, woman and so on, or basic concepts such as top, bottom or middle. Clearly such written symbols were inadequate, and in time separate individual items were joined together to form a new character, to express an idea that could not be described pictorially. Thus there is a character for roof and a character for woman, place one over the other and you have one woman under one roof, which means peace.

Other simple examples include: a man standing by the character for speech meaning a written missive, the sun and the moon together mean brightness, two trees mean a wood, three trees mean a forest, a bird and a mouth mean to sing, strength and field mean male and many more. But of course this too was inadequate as society advanced, and in time more and more characters had to be invented, often quite arbitrarily, or if there was a logic it is no longer discernible today. Characters, or parts of characters, were combined in various juxtapositions to create totally new ones; the radical or prime part denoting sometimes the general field of meaning, what is misleadingly called the phonetic, which only sometimes give the sound. Scholars have published analyses of the common written characters, showing the various component parts. They are of little help to would-be students. The only way to learn written Chinese is by endless practise, writing the same character over and over again. The Chinese language with its ramifications relates equally to all literate Chinese be they from China or South-East Asia. A good hand and knowledge of the classics is respected in both Singapore and Peking.

The uniformity of the written does not extend to the spoken. The major dialects, while having roughly common roots and word order, are mostly mutually unintelligible; indeed they can in extreme cases be as far apart as, say, French and Spanish. A northerner from Peking, whose native speech is Putonghua, the common tongue, known in the West as Mandarin, cannot understand Cantonese or other southeastern seaboard dialects such as those of Xiamen or Fuzhou, all common throughout Nanyang. He will also take quite a long time, many months, to learn them even adequately. He will understand a little Shanghainese and other Yangzi river basin dialects as these are closer. His interlocutors from the provinces will however mostly understand him and be able to reply in Mandarin, albeit accented, as this is now the national language, a symbol of unity, the lingua franca for all Chinese wherever they may be, taught since the 1950s in schools throughout non-Mandarin speaking areas in China and now increasingly outside it. A peculiarity common to all these Chinese spoken dialects is the paucity of homonyms or different sounds; there are only about 400 in Mandarin, for example. Over time a tonal system evolved thus increasing the range of sounds; each major dialect has from four to nine such tones, in one case arguably twelve. Mandarin, the common tongue, has four; thus 1,600 different sounds, still not many, as against about three times the number in English. The bizarre situation will arise whereby several written characters, all different in construction and meaning will share an identical sound and tone and so if read out loud, separately and not in context, may lead to confusion and misunderstanding. In practice, modern spoken and written Chinese is largely made up of compounds whereby meaning is confirmed by linkage and context. This also means the speaker from another province whose tones are inaccurate, or the foreign student who cannot master them, can usually, but not always, be understood. When the possibility of misunderstanding exists, Chinese will sometimes write the character or even trace it on the palm of the listener's hand.

The majority of the Han population are native Mandarin speakers, albeit with varying regional accents. There are however no class accents in China, in that sense all speak the same. The purest, or most correct form is Peking Mandarin, and the best would probably be spoken by a native of the city who is a graduate of the university. It is a pleasant, lilting tongue and speakers roll their r's, so when they speak English they sound American. As stated, most Northern Chinese Mandarin speakers have considerable difficulty learning the Southern dialects, chiefly due to pronunciation and the greater number of tones. The next major dialect, actually a language in its own right, is Cantonese, centred on Guangdong province; Guangdong means Broad East and encompasses Hong Kong and Macao as well. It is also spoken in parts of the neighbouring province of Guangxi, Broad West, and throughout Overseas Chinese settlements in South-East Asia. It is the first language of over 80 million people and its purest form is spoken in the provincial capital of Canton, with very considerable variations throughout the region. North of Macao is the Toishan dialect which in San Francisco Chinatown is still spoken in its late 18th century form, a legacy of the earliest settlements on the west coast of the USA. Nearby are the Four Districts, again with a distinct dialect, then there are the Hoklo, the Tanka who are boat people, also the people of Swatow to the north of the province. As you travel away from the epicentre, west, or south, or north, so the local speech gets further away from its standard form. On the East river, north of the Hong Kong border, are to be found the Hakka, speaking a very different dialect stemming from their original home in North China, whence they came 1,000 years ago. Most Nanyang Huaqiao are Cantonese speakers, closely followed by Hokkien from Fujian up the coast, others include Teochew, Hakka, Hailam, Foochow.

The fundamental structure of Cantonese is the same as for Mandarin, as indeed is the case with the other main Chinese languages. However, not only are Cantonese and Mandarin mutually unintelligible due to the very widely differing pronunciation but there are nine tones in Cantonese; so if it is easy to get it wrong in Mandarin it is easier still to get it wrong in Cantonese. Cantonese learn to speak Mandarin readily and now in increasing numbers in Hong Kong, particularly since the handover to China in 1997; a south to north conversion course takes about three months. But Cantonese have a distinctive accent and get certain common sounds wrong, including even day to day expressions such as to eat, or number four. Similar differences exist between the other major Chinese dialects spoken in Nanyang; all are to very varying degree mutually unintelligible, though have the same fundamental structure. Inevitably all now have numerous loan words from the country of adoption, which makes their speech sometimes difficult to understand for their compatriots back home in China. Thus for example the word for soap in Malay is 'sabun' and this has entered the Chinese vocabulary too. In fact the original Chinese word for soap has been lost in Malaysia; visiting Chinese from other regions have a hard time trying to buy it. By the same token, Chinese dialect words have been transmogrified into local language; the Malay towkay, boss or merchant originally comes from Hokkien, the Indonesian tjukong, pillar or backer is Cantonese, as is kongsi, company or enterprise. Those that speak Mandarin do so with a distinct accent that, as well as their appearance, betrays their origin immediately.

Nanyang Chinese English is about the same as the English spoken by the locals throughout the region. It is accented to varying degree, in Indonesia with a rolling r, in Singapore and Malaysia often with a 'lah' at the end of every sentence. In the Philippines it is fluent American accented English with a few Tagalog words thrown in, in Thailand sometimes there is a slight singsong. (Cantonese sometimes give tones to English words). The word order and syntax of this Nanyang English is special. Prepositions are often omitted entirely, or wrongly used and tenses are seldom varied. The most common is the present continuous: thus, 'I am waiting my friend'. Sometimes a sentence lacks an object or a subject. Those with a fanciful turn of mind say you can detect Chinese grammar and word order in all this, or perhaps, the influence of the regional languages. There are numerous examples of what could almost be called a dialect: If surprised or perplexed you never say, 'how can this be?' but, 'how can?' So it goes on. Many Westernised Nanyang Chinese speak English of this sort to each other, fluently and frequently, often interlarded with local vocabulary or Chinese dialect. They have sometimes a little difficulty in following standard homeside (another word) English and would be lost reading the Times. But these remarks apply only to some. Many speak flawless, erudite English and are conversant with our literature and history as well. Another feature of the region is the linguistic ability of the population of whatever race. It is common to find ordinary villagers in poor rural districts switching from native dialect to very different national language and back, with fluency and facility.

Nearly all Huaqiao speak more than one language, sometimes three or more: their native dialect, the language of their adopted country and now increasingly, Mandarin. Those that have had a Chinese style education are also of course literate in their language and use it all the time; those who were not brought up to read and write Chinese mostly have a poor command, if any, of the characters. There are long established communities which have been largely culturally assimilated by their country of adoption. In some cases they speak no Chinese at all even to each other, let alone read or write it (they are known by the slang term of 'hollow bamboo'). A large proportion of the population of all races speaks English, the international business lingua franca of the region. The incidence of Dutch, French, Portuguese or Spanish, all previous colonial languages, has declined of course drastically; the few that still speak them are invariably old. The standard of all languages, including Chinese, spoken by Huaqiao varies as much as their provenance and their background.

7

The Spice Route: The Early Economy of South-East Asia

Economics and politics have always been closely linked together in South-East Asia, even more so than in the West. The political and cultural development of the region, including the Chinese migration and settlement described in the first half of this book, have had a strong impact on the economies and business cultures of the region, and continue to do so. At the same time, business and commerce, especially trade with China and with the West, have in turn helped shape the politics and culture of the region. To understand the history of South-East Asia, it is also necessary to understand its economy – and vice versa.

In the second half of this book we turn to matters of trade, economy and business culture. We begin with a short history of the economy of the region up to the 1990s, and show how long distance trade, colonial domination and independence coincide with three separate phases in economic development. In all three of these phases, the Chinese of Nanyang have played a role.

The first phase we will discuss, when South-East Asia's economy was dominated by long-distance trade with China, India, the Arab world and Western Europe, is by far the longest. We do not really know when this trade began; certainly it was in existence for many centuries before the birth of Christ. Spices from South-East Asia were known to the ancient Chinese and the ancient Egyptians alike; resins and perfumes of South-East Asian origin have been found in the tombs of the pharaohs. There is even a suggestion that some of the pharaohs were interested in developing direct trade, rather than relying on Indian middlemen. One pharaoh, probably Neko II (610–595 BC), sent out an exploring party of Phoenician sailors, who circumnavigated Africa looking for the 'Spice Islands' in the mistaken belief that they lay to the south rather than the east.

Doubt has been cast on whether this circumnavigation actually took place (although, as one authority has commented, if it did not happen, then how did people know that Africa could be circumnavigated?), but certainly the ancient civilisations of the Mediterranean and Middle East were aware of South-East Asia and its riches, even if they were not always very clear where the so-called Spice Islands were. Herodotus mentions the spice trade, and so do later Greek and Roman geographers. The Roman Empire provided a large and rich market for eastern products, as did the rising new states of north India such as the Mauryan kingdom of Chandragupta and his successors. And, of course, roughly coincident with the rise of Rome came the rise of unified China under the Qin and Han dynasties. With growing markets for its products across Asia, the Middle East and Europe, South-East Asia suddenly became an important economic centre.

Contemporary observers and modern historians alike often refer to the 'spice trade', but this is a simple name for a complex trade in hundreds of products. Of course spices were an important part of the trade. Some, like nutmeg, were indigenous to the region; nutmeg in particular came originally from a few small islands in the Molucca (Maluku) group in modern Indonesia. Others were more common, but South-East Asia was still regarded as the best source. The most common spice, traded in the largest bulk to both China and the West, was pepper. Medieval trade manifests identify more than a hundred different kinds of pepper, ranging from the black peppercorns and white peppercorns which we are familiar with today, to others that seem to have resembled what we now call chilis. Other kinds of peppers listed cannot be identified today, and it is possible that they have disappeared entirely.

South-East Asian pepper dominated the long-distance trade, especially with the West. No estimate has ever been made of the quantities carried, and the total value of the trade can only be guessed at. Alexandria under Arab rule had an entire market, the *Shari al-Filih*, Pepper Street, dedicated to the trade in this single group of products. In the primitive stock exchanges, or bourses, of Genoa and Venice and Bruges, it was possible to buy and sell pepper futures. Pepper could even serve as currency; in England, the term 'peppercorn rent' still exists, commemorating a time when ground rents could be paid in pepper. The wealth generated by this trade was phenomenal. The risks were high, but the profits were higher still. One Venetian merchant reckoned he could send five ships to buy pepper in Alexandria, and even if four of them sank in storms or were captured by pirates, the profit from the fifth cargo would more than offset his losses.

Spices aside, the tropical forests of South-East Asia produced many other products that the rest of the world needed. Drugs were an important commodity especially in the trade with China, where along with more dubious products such as tigers' penises, there developed a trade in aromatic herbs and roots thought to have medicinal properties. Incense was also a valuable export to China and India. Even more important was the trade in dyes, vital for the burgeoning textile industries of both China and Western Europe. By about 1400, the woods and herbs used for making dyes, sandalwood being one of the most prominent, probably accounted for second place in the European trade, after pepper.

The importance of this trade to the people of South-East Asia, of course, was relative. Most of the population of South-East Asia still made their living from agriculture and fishing. Control of production of spices, aromatics, incense, dyewoods and other valuable products was in the hands of local chieftains and potentates, who exploited these for the benefit of themselves and their families and retinues. Chinese Marxist historians call this the 'feudal period', and the description is in some ways apt. Certainly wealth was not distributed. The local potentates sold to middlemen in the seaports, who in turn sold to the sea-going merchants who came calling; these in turn transported the cargoes at their own risk, and sold the goods in their home ports. As noted above, these merchants, regardless of nationality, assumed the lion's share of the risk, and therefore took the greater part of the profit.

Although China was far closer than the West, the China trade never developed into a major factor in the local economy. Partly, of course, China had its own tropical and sub-tropical regions which could produce some of the same products. China did, as noted in earlier chapters, interfere politically in the region from time to time, and its periods of political domination of Annam and Cochin (in what is now Vietnam) coincided with attempts by Chinese merchants to capture the trade of those regions. The beginnings of permanent Chinese emigration into other parts of South-East Asia also helped to stimulate trade with China, but only to a limited extent.

China was an uncertain market. During periods of (relative) stability such as the Han dynasty (206 BC–220 AD) or the Tang dynasty (618–907 AD), China was prosperous and there was a stronger demand for luxury goods such as incense, spices dyes and drugs. The Mongol conquest of China in the 13th century initially meant disruption, but the Mongol rulers of the Yuan dynasty (1271–1368), Kubilai Khan and his successors, tried to stimulate trade and eradicate piracy in the South China Sea and the East Indies. The successors of the Yuan, the Ming dynasty, followed this policy at first. Then, suddenly in around the middle of the 15th century, the Ming dynasty seemed to lose interest in anything outside of China, with the result that piracy increased and trade began to wane again. By this time, another power was poised to make an entrance on the scene.

The damage caused by piracy should not be overestimated. Japan, poor and politically disorganised, had long been a haven for pirates, and from the 12th century onward Japanese pirates raided the coast of China and as far south as the Indonesian archipelago. Some believe it was their depredations that caused some local tribes, notably the Sea-Dyaks of western Borneo, to turn to piracy themselves. Kubilai Khan famously led a fleet against Japan in the 13th century to try to suppress this menace, but his fleet was destroyed by a storm, the *Kamikaze* or Divine Wind that has gone down in Japanese history. The 15th century saw piracy increase as Japan became still more unstable. The terrible civil conflicts of the 16th century, still known to Japanese historians as the Age of the Nation at War, sent many Japanese into exile. Some found work as mercenaries for local sultans and warlords in South-East Asia, while others resorted to piracy. The Japanese pirates whom the British and Dutch traders encountered, and fought, in the seas around Sumatra in the early 17th century were probably descendants of these exiles. Their primary field of activity, however, was in the South China sea and around the Philippines, where they burned towns and cities, terrorised local populations and at times managed to almost completely block trade.

All these factors, uncertain markets, political instability and piracy, meant that over the course of about a thousand years, roughly from 600 to 1600 AD, South-East Asia's overseas trade became more and more directed towards the West. As noted in Chapter 2, Indian sailors and merchants began reaching the region in ever-increasing numbers. India's growing wealth and population during this period meant that India itself was a strong market. But India was also strongly established as an entrepot in east-west trade – the early silk trade with Western Europe, for example, passed south of the Himalayas through northern India, not north of them through Central Asia as in later years. Indian merchants dominated the trade for a long time, and left their own mark on the region's culture.

Following the establishment of the Islamic caliphate in the 7th century, Arab traders began arriving in the region. At first their numbers were small, but they soon became important players in the local economy. The big Arab sea-going dhows could handle all but the toughest monsoon conditions in the Indian Ocean, and the Arab traders soon gained the necessary experience of local winds and currents. As well as trade the Arabs also brought the message of Islam, which spread first among the educated upper classes and gradually to the lower orders. This in turn engendered a sense of community, which was itself good for trade. In the east, new trading centres sprang to prominence. The most important were Malacca on the southwest coast of the Malay peninsula, about a hundred miles northwest of modern Singapore, and Aceh (modern Banda Aceh) on the northwestern tip of Sumatra. Both were ruled by Muslim sultans who welcomed their co-religionists trading from across the sea. Both became rich places, and with wealth came culture. Aceh in particular became one of the centres of learning in the Muslim world under the influence of the Indian-born scholar and theologian Nur al-Din al-Raniri, who helped to spread the ideas of the mystical branch of Islam known as Sufism throughout the region. Aceh's *madrassis* (religious schools) produced a number of important and influential Islamic scholars.

The ports of south India such as Goa and Calicut continued to be important, but new ports also came to prominence further west, Hormuz and Muscat controlling the mouth of the Persian Gulf, Aden at the mouth of the Red Sea. The sultans of these places, like those of Malacca and Aceh, grew rich. We have no accurate data on the volume of the trade, but from the relative ease with which scholars, pilgrims and travellers passed back and forth from the Middle East to South-East Asia, the traffic must have been considerable.

On reaching the Middle East from South-East Asia, the trade divided. Some went from Aden up the Red Sea, where goods were transshipped and carried by camel to the Mediterranean. Pepper and other goods were then carried by local boats to ports such as Alexandria, where Arab middlemen sold them on to merchants from Western Europe, usually from one of the big Italian ports such as Venice, Genoa or Pisa. From these latter ports, Italian merchants distributed the products of South-East Asia all over southern and western Europe. Meanwhile, the trade from Hormuz and Muscat continued on up the Persian Gulf and then up the Tigris and Euphrates Rivers. Some merchants then went overland to Syria and its Mediterranean ports such as Antioch or Acre, from whence goods followed the same trajectory as above. Others continued on to the southern coast of the Black Sea, from whence more ships carried the precious cargoes across to the northern shore, to ports such as Kilia, now in Romania, and Akkerman, now in Moldova. From here the great rivers of eastern Europe, the Danube and the Dniestr, served as highways carrying trade into the central European interior. A few more transhipments and goods were being freighted by boat down the Elbe and the Vistula to reach the Baltic. A humble nutmeg, travelling from the islands of the Moluccas to a market in London, would have come halfway around the world and been on a journey greater than any person at the time could imagine.

Or, not quite. Since the 9th century, if not before, Arab geographers had been compiling travellers' reports and slowly assembling a body of knowledge – not always accurate – about South-East Asia. During the so-called renaissance of the 12th century, when hundreds of Arabic books were translated into Latin, the Western European imagination became charged with images of the East, not just South-East Asia but China and Japan too. Some people began to realise that opening a direct trade route to the east offered chances for profit. Explorers began setting out. Two Genoese navigators, the brothers Vivaldi, set off down the west coast of Africa at the end of the 13th century, looking for a sea route to the east. They never returned, but the idea that Asia could be reached by sea persisted. Others travelled overland, from Syria and the Black Sea east through Central Asia and Persia. Karakorum, then capital of the Mongol Empire, was reached in the middle of the 13th century by the Franciscan friar Giovanni Pian del Carpini; he found there was already a flourishing little community of European traders and craftsmen established in the city. A few years later, two Venetian merchants, the brothers Niccolò and Maffeo Polo penetrated still further east. Returning home, they recruited backers for a new journey, this time famously taking with them the young Marco Polo.

Marco Polo's account of his 20 years in the Far East is a fascinating mixture of fact and fantasy, so much so that some have wondered whether he was a fraud who never made the journey at all and merely compiled rumours and accounts of other travellers. But it must be remembered that Polo himself did not write the account of his journeys that we now read. It was told by him to one Rusticello of Pisa, a writer of romantic fiction, who wrote it down and published it. Rusticello was interested in telling a good yarn, and so the marital customs of the Indians and the attractiveness of Chinese prostitutes figure more largely in his narrative than does the price of tea. But there seems little doubt that the journeys of the Polos greatly increased knowledge about East and South-East Asia, especially on the part of the merchant classes. Slowly and steadily, the merchants of the German and Italian cities moved east, working their way along the trade routes. By the end of the 15th century, Venetian traders had permanent stations at several cities in Persia and were frequent visitors to India.

However, they were beaten in the race to the Spice Islands by a small and hitherto unregarded nation: Portugal. From the middle of the 15th century, stimulated by that remarkable figure known as Prince Henry the Navigator, Portuguese ships had been setting out from the port of Lagos trying to find a way around Africa. Progress was slow. Some ships were lost in storms, others attacked by hostile locals off West Africa. A belt of contrary winds around the equator seemed to present an impassable barrier, until it was discovered that it was possible to sail across the Atlantic to Brazil, touch there at Recife or Pernambuco to take on water and food, and then sail back across to the coast of southern Africa to what is now Angola. In 1488, Bartolomew Diaz became the first European navigator to round the Cape of Storms (now Cape of Good Hope), the southern tip of Africa. Ten years later, Vasco da Gama's expedition reached southern India.

The news of da Gama's expedition shocked Europe, much more so than Columbus's apparently fruitless expedition to the Caribbean six years earlier. The Italian merchant cities realised that their domination of the eastern trade was ended. The Venetian stock market crashed. Wild plans were drawn up to dig a canal across the Suez peninsula to link the Mediterranean with the Red Sea. In Portugal, a new expedition set out led by Pedro Cabral, with the intention of establishing a permanent presence in the East. A later expedition followed, led by the dynamic viceroy Afonso de Albuquerque. Aden and Hormuz were seized for use as way stations, and to cut off Arab control of the trade. More colonies were established in Angola, Brazil and Mozambique, originally to provide havens for ships travelling to and from the east. After a number of battles with local princes, the Portuguese seized the port of Goa and made it their base in India.

From there they spread rapidly east. Albuquerque sacked the ancient and rich port of Malacca in 1511 and made it the capital of the Portuguese empire in the Far East. Within a few years Portuguese ships were sailing throughout the Indonesian archipelago, establishing enclaves such as Dili in what is now East Timor. Further afield they established trading posts at Macao in southern China and even, despite the civil war raging in the country at the time, at Nagasaki in Japan.

The pattern established by the Portuguese would be followed by other European powers in the centuries to come. The Portuguese were not interested in occupation; their main aim was to control as much of the trade as possible. This meant control of the seas rather than the land. Where possible, they did deals with local sultans and princes; where not, as in the case of Malacca, they used military force to quell opposition. There were now three key sets of players in the trade: the sultans and princes, who owned the land and the productive resources; the Portuguese, who had largely taken over the carrying trade; and the middlemen of the towns. The Portuguese, who were of course staunch Roman Catholics, preferred not to do business directly with the local Muslims; they had been fighting against Muslims for centuries in their homeland, and there were strong prejudices still. Increasingly these middlemen – *compradores*, as the Portuguese called them – were drawn from the Chinese populations of the towns and cities. These were experienced traders who, with the Chinese market slowly declining, were eager to seize new opportunities. It is almost certainly from these *compradores* that the Portuguese seamen and traders learned about the opportunities to be had in China; it may well have been a south Chinese migrant who guided the first Portuguese ships to Macao at the mouth of the Pearl River.

This symbiosis worked well. The Portuguese empire could not and did not last; a nation of three million could not hope to sustain such an enterprise. But other European powers were ready to follow in her footsteps. The Magellan expedition established, as related in Chapter 4, a Spanish presence in the Philippines that would last for several centuries. Sir Francis Drake's *Golden Hind* passed through the region late in the 16th century, and although her hold was already full of tons of gold and silver looted from the Spanish colony in Peru, the canny Drake stopped and bought as much nutmeg as could be crammed aboard. Later, when the ship ran aground and some of the cargo needed to be jettisoned, Drake ordered that some of the silver be thrown overboard but the bags of nutmegs should be saved; proof if proof were needed of the value that spices could command in European markets. English interest in the region was now established. The Portuguese empire collapsed at the end of the 16th century, but by then England and the Netherlands were both preparing to take Portugal's place.

The struggle for control of the South-East Asian trade between the English and Dutch East India Companies has been told often, and needs only a bare summary here. The English arrived first, and initially had some success in taking over the trade from the Portuguese, establishing their own posts at Aceh and then further east into the Indonesian archipelago; several unpleasant brushes with pirates seem to have dissuaded them from pushing further north. The Dutch East India

Company, founded in 1602, was soon competing with the English. This was a trade war, which quite frequently turned into a shooting war. The ships and men of both sides were heavily armed, and clashes were common with plenty of blood shed on both sides. For a time the English station in Aceh was literally under siege by local forces in the pay of the Dutch. At sea, when not engaged in trade, ships of both companies went in search of each other looking for a fight. One later historian complained of the difficulties of distinguishing between trading ships, official warships and ships engaged in piracy at this time, and suggested that all three activities might be usefully subsumed into a single term, 'armed violence at sea'.

In 1613 the energetic young Dutch factor Jan Pieterszoon Coen was appointed to control the Dutch stations on the island of Java, and within a few years had driven the English, often forcibly, off the island. In 1618 Coen was appointed governor-general of the Dutch Company and effectively given a free hand in the East Indies. Within a further four years he had expelled the English Company from all of its posts in the East, with the single exception of Aceh. In 1624 he acquired Malacca from the Portuguese, and by the time of his death in 1629 he had – with a dozen ships and a few hundred men – cemented Dutch control over the Indonesian archipelago, and control the sea-going trade of the entire region. The English East India Company then turned its attentions to India instead. Although English traders began developing a trade with south China in the early 17th century, they steered clear of Dutch ports and islands and had little presence in South-East Asia.

The Dutch, on the other hand, dominated the commerce of the region from the early 17th century to the beginning of the 19th century. Like the Portuguese, they were initially interested in control of the ports and the ocean-going trade. As time went on, they gradually took control of more and more of the islands as well, especially the fertile agricultural lands of Java and eastern Sumatra. Immigrants began arriving from Holland and settling, mostly in the towns, and gradually the East Indies became a colony. But, even though the Dutch were gradually taking control of the productive resources – farms, timber, mines – the role of the Chinese remained as important as ever. Like the Portuguese, the Dutch colonialists were few in number; they needed skilled business brains to help them run their enterprises, particularly ones who could speak the local languages. Chinese control over the mercantile activities of the towns positively increased under Dutch colonial rule. The negative aspect of this was that in the minds of many Indonesian *pribumis*, the Chinese were associated with colonial rule, and were complicit in that rule.

This state of affairs lasted until the Napoleonic Wars broke out in Europe at the very end of the 18th century. Back in Europe, the Netherlands were occupied by the French, but the Dutch East Indies remained by and large unaffected until very late in the war, when a brief French occupation of Java was followed by a brief British one. There were other naval skirmishes between French and British warships, with local Dutch occasionally involved, but on the whole the local Dutch authorities tried to remain neutral. But the uncertainty and lack of governmental control from Europe meant that there were now opportunities for traders from other nations. The end of the Napoleonic Wars saw the Netherlands firmly in the Allied camp – Dutch troops played a prominent role in the defeat of Napoleon at Waterloo – and inclined to be co-operative where Far Eastern matters were concerned. The doors to the South-East Asian trade were opened. The British East India Company, now dominant in India, began probing east again. Singapore was acquired in 1819, and Malacca, still a useful port though no longer dominant, in 1824, laying the foundation for the Straits Settlements. These ports began to be used as way stations for the growing trade between British India and China; including, of course, the export of opium from the former to the latter. The British company's permanent establishment at Hong Kong from 1841 confirmed British interest not only in China, but all across the region. By the midde of the century, American traders were arriving in the Philippines, and French merchants were in Vietnam and Cambodia while Britain consolidated its trading interests in the Malay peninsula and began to encroach from India into Burma.

As yet, though, the economy was still largely based on the export of luxury goods: spices, dyes, tropical hardwoods, aromatics and incense. But major change was coming. The Industrial Revolution had now spread across Europe, and the new industrialising economies needed raw materials. Resource-rich South-East Asia could provide these. The new colonial regimes in the region wanted timber, copra, palm oil, jute and above all, rubber and oil. And, in order to extract these resources, the colonial powers needed to control the land. Until now, the Europeans had remained concentrated in towns and along the coasts. Now they spread out to take control of the entire region. There was bloody fighting in some cases. In Borneo it took several generations to finally suppress the Sea-Dyak pirates. In Annam, Chinese-backed resistance forces handed the French several defeats in the 1880s before resistance finally ceased, and in Burma, three wars and a long campaign against bandits were needed to bring the country under British control. The seizure of the Philippines by the Americans from the Spanish in 1898 provoked a ten-year-long rebellion. But by 1900, only Thailand had not become a colony – a fact which helps to explain why even today, Thailand's economy is slightly different from those of the rest of the region.

Oil was probably the salvation of the increasingly moribund Dutch colony. Oil was needed as a machine lubricant in the factories of the west and also, increasingly, to provide fuel for automobiles and, as oil-fired engines began replacing coal-fired steam engines, for navies and merchant ships. The Royal Dutch Petroleum company was established to exploit this resource but soon ran into stiff competition from the British-based Shell Transport and Trading Company. But in 1900 Royal Dutch appointed the 34 year old Henri Deterding, formerly the sales manager for the Sumatra region, as managing director. Deterding understood how to exploit the burgeoning European market. Production increased, and Rotterdam became one of the largest oil terminals in Europe. By 1907, Deterding and Royal Dutch had driven Marcus Samuel's Shell Transport and Trading almost to the wall. The two companies merged to form the Royal Dutch/Shell group, but with Deterding and Royal Dutch very much in control. Royal Dutch/Shell went on to become one of the three most powerful oil companies in the world, along with Standard Oil of the USA and the Anglo-Persian Company (now BP). It remains one of the giants of the oil industry.

The establishment of rubber plantations in Malaya and later in Burma, Indonesia and the French colonies transformed the South-East Asian economy. Rubber was another vital component of industrialisation. Tyres, first for bicycles and then for automobiles, were in great demand, but rubber had many other industrial applications as well. It was also discovered that it was easier to control the quality of plantation rubber than the so-called 'wild' rubber tapped from the forests of South America. While oil was a powerful economic force, the rubber industry changed not just the economy but also society and even the landscape, as wide areas of jungle were cleared to make way for the plantations. Rubber production was also labour-intensive, and required the importation of labour, particularly from China.

Other vegetable products, primarily fibres and oils, proved to have strong demand. Copra, the dried meat of the coconut, was a major export; the oil derived from copra was important in the food industry. So too was palm oil, required by the rapidly growing soap industry.

Lever Brothers set the pace by establishing palm oil plantations in the Solomon Islands, but soon it and other companies were setting up plantations in Burma and Malaya. Jute, used in making sacking and ropes, was another important export, as was kapok, which was used among many other things for filling life-preserving vests for sailors. Tropical hardwoods, especially teak, were in high demand; in the late 19th and early 20th centuries, warships and passenger liners built with steel hulls often continued to have teak decks. The naval arms race before World War I required tens of thousands of tons of teak decking. Tin and bauxite were also mined, and Burma's mines produced rubies, some suitable for cutting as gems, most used in industrial applications as cutting tools. Even such agricultural staples as rice were shipped to Europe and America to help feed rapidly growing populations. The growing trade also led to a massive expansion of shipping in Western Europe especially, and this in turn required a rapid expansion of the shipbuilding industry. The historian C. Northcote Parkinson, in his book *The Trade Winds*, has also shown how the trade led to a huge expansions of port capacity, notably in places such as Rotterdam and London, but in smaller centres too. The little Scottish port of Dundee became known as Jute City for its reliance on the jute trade. And all these industries provided work and created wealth, and this in turn stimulated further demand for imports.

During this period, the relative balance of economic power changed in South-East Asia. The indigenous Vietnamese and Malays and Indonesians had now lost control. European – and in the Philippines, American – colonial governments controlled the economy, and European and American businesses dominated resource extraction and the export trade. However, it suited the colonial masters to leave the structure of Chinese small traders, middlemen and wholesalers largely intact. The Chinese traders increased their own economic power, albeit often very marginally, at the expense of the indigenous populations. Chinese family firms controlled local banking and moneylending markets, for example, and in most countries were the predominant owners of local shops. Some Chinese trading houses became very wealthy, especially in Malaya and Thailand.

The collapse of the Chinese empire brought a fresh flood of migrants. But ironically, this also brought new trading opportunities for existing businesses, who used both the new migrants and existing family networks to re-establish contact with the mother country. They were encouraged to do so by Chiang Kai-shek's government. His prime minister and finance minister, T.V. Soong, encouraged the wealthy Chinese of Nanyang to support his government. In 1936, it was estimated that 60% of the Nationalist government's direct revenue (not counting subventions from the American government) came from donations from the Chinese community outside of China.

This should not be taken to mean that all the Chinese of Nanyang were prosperous, however. Many did do well, but many more lived and worked in poverty alongside the local population. Earlier, we noted how Chinese workers were recruited to work on the labour-intensive rubber plantations across the region, and likewise they were recruited to work on the oil wells in Indonesia. The myth of the 'rich Chinese' became unhappily analogous with the European myth of the 'rich Jew', and in some cases, with the same tragic consequences.

It was not only the Europeans and the Americans who needed South-East Asia's resources. In 1868, the year the Meiji Emperor came to the throne and began Japan's economic reform, the country was technologically backward and extremely poor. Within 30 years, Japan was on the brink of full industrialisation. The speed and scale of the change is in some ways analogous to that of China today; Japan is a far smaller country with fewer people, but Japan also had further to travel to catch up with the West. Under the Shoguns, Japan had been deliberately isolated and technology had regressed. For example, firearms, once common in Japanese armies, had been banned; in 1868, bows and swords were the standard weapon of the Japanese army. But less than 30 years later, a modern Japanese army and fleet had evicted the Chinese from Taiwan and Korea, and just a few years after that, in 1904–05, Japan defeated the Russian Empire and seized control of Manchuria.

Important though Taiwan, Korea and Manchuria were for supporting Japan's growing industrial economy and rising population, they were not enough. Japan needed the same things the West did, especially oil and rubber, and the closest sources of these were in South-East Asia. In the years after World War I, Japanese society and politics became increasingly militarised; the emperors were sidelined once again, and the army and navy controlled the government. The economic interests of Japan were the economic interests of the army and navy. Plans were laid for a 'Greater East Asia Co-Prosperity Sphere', which was touted abroad as being an attempt to give the Asian peoples more economic control and prosperity, but was in fact the blueprint for a Japanese empire in the Far East.

It is therefore unsurprising that Japan's entry into World War II saw immediate attacks on British and Dutch colonies in South-East Asia.

The retreating Dutch blew up their oil wells, but the Japanese quickly salvaged them and pressed local workers back into service. The abandoned Malayan rubber estates were also quickly put back into working order. The French colonies in Vietnam, Cambodia and Laos were supposedly neutral, the Vichy government in France having signed a peace treaty with Japan's ally Germany, but the Japanese commanders overran these also before going on to occupy Burma. Thailand, likewise neutral, was occupied without a struggle. The region and its economy were now under Japanese control.

Fortunately, that control did not last long. For the Chinese of Nanyang, this was a terrible time. Racist attitudes among the Japanese troops meant that the Chinese were treated very harshly. Chinese shops and businesses were looted, and many thousands killed outright. In some countries, notably Burma and Indonesia, where there had already been bad blood, locals either stood by or joined in the looting and killing. But then the end of the war came and the Japanese empire collapsed. However, this was by no means the end of Japanese economic involvement in the region, as we shall see in the next chaper.

The third phase of economic development began with the postwar independence movements, as described in Chapters 3 and 4. At this point there occurs a kind of economic fragmentation of the region, with each country following its own trajectory. That trajectory was largely dependent on the political situation. On one end of the scale were those countries like Thailand, Malaysia, Indonesia and above all, Singapore, where free market ideology ran strongest. These countries might be characterised by political uncertainty; Thailand and Indonesia certainly were, and as we noted in Chapter 4 the fall of the Sukarno government was accompanied by repressive measures aimed at the Chinese community. But they still remained 'open for business' and attempted to attract foreign direct investment, with varying degrees of success. At the other end of the scale were those countries that developed communist regimes, Vietnam, Laos and, for a brief and terrible time, Cambodia. Here economic development shuddered to a halt. Vietnam did undertake a much needed programme of land reform in the late 1950s which helped redistribute wealth, but the Vietnam war rolled back any economic gains that might have been made. In between were countries such as Burma and the Philippines, in the grip of corrupt dictatorships and gently stagnating from the 1950s to the 1970s.

World War II and the subsequent struggles for independence had done much damage to infrastructure and industry. Again with

Singapore excepted, every country lacked skilled engineers, technicians and civil servants. The lack was even more apparent amongst the indigenous populations, who by and large had less access to education than did the Chinese. People who had no experience of running an economy were thrust into positions of power with responsibility for the economic welfare of many millions. Mistakes were made, like Indonesia's ill-starred nationalisation of all Dutch-owned businesses in the 1950s. Without their skilled Dutch owners and managers, many of these businesses crumbled. Only in Singapore and Malaysia during this period is there evidence of anything like systematic economic planning. Military dictatorships, communist regimes and democratic republics alike were eventually forced to come to terms with the need to work with their Chinese 'guests'. The latter were the only group with the ability to revive the moribund economies of the region.

A word needs to be said about two of the regions' economies, Thailand and Singapore, in this twilight period between the end of World War II and the start of the modern economic boom. For several decades, Singapore was the exception to the South-East Asian rule. Thanks in part to the visionary leadership of the little state's founders, and thanks to the work ethic and open-mindedness of its largely Chinese population, Singapore prospered from the beginning. Having an open economy that would attract investment was seen as a key to survival. Singapore positioned itself as a 'safe haven' for multi-national companies seeking a base in South-East Asia, somewhere where they could establish head offices, set up bank accounts and the launch out into the risky and uncertain environment around. Many European, American and Japanese companies took advantage of this offering. As a result, from an early date, Singapore's managers and workers became exposed to other management cultures and ideas, and proved themselves adept at taking these on and adapting them to their own work.

Singapore became the financial capital of South-East Asia, and was for a time even spoken of seriously as a rival to Hong Kong and Tokyo. It built a reputation for probity and transparency, unlike other stock markets in the region. Unquestionably, Singapore aspired to economic leadership in South-East Asia, to become the 'brain' that would direct the 'hands' of the poorer nations around. To some extent this has happened. Yet for all Singapore's economic clout, the country to watch over the years has been Thailand. Its history has mirrored the history of the whole region in many ways, and even today, watching Thailand can give clues about the problems – and opportunities – to be found in the region.

Thailand did not have a struggle for independence, of course, because it had not been colonised. Yet in the early days after World War II it was affected by the same malaise as the countries around it. Political uncertainty at home and abroad affected development. A right-wing military dictatorship strongly allied to the USA controlled the country until the early 1960s, and even after a constitutional monarchy was re-established, the army continued – and continues – to play a major role in the economy and politics alike. The 1950s saw a few hesitant moves by foreign companies into Thailand, and the gradual building of links between Thai companies – many owned and run by ethnic Chinese, although these tended by and large to take Thai names – and other companies around the region, especially in Malaysia and Singapore.

While the Vietnam War was economically disastrous for Vietnam, Cambodia and Laos, it did provide some benefits for Thailand. US military presence was not an unmixed blessing – sharp rises in drug trafficking and prostitution were among its consequences. But that presence was also accompanied by generous helpings of aid money, and enough wealth was distributed around the country to begin priming the pump. The Thai economy started to stir. Larger-scale businesses began to merge, like Bangkok Bank, headed by the Thai-born Chinese banker Chin Sophanpanich. Bangkok Bank in turn backed other firms, including notably the agriculture and animal feed company Charoen Pokphand, owned by an immigrant family from Shantou district. In the 1970s, as the Vietnam conflicts finally ended, Thailand began attracting interest from more foreign multi-national companies, especially Japanese firms. Gradually its more free market-oriented neighbours began attracting more interest too.

While the 1970s was in general a decade of recession, it was for parts of South-East Asia, at least, a decade of awakening. At least some countries were showing signs of economic growth, fuelled by a combination of foreign investment and the rising strength of a few domestic firms, very often Chinese-owned and managed. The story of how that growth transformed and then nearly wrecked South Asia will be told in the next chapter.

8
The Rise and Fall of the Tigers

In 1960, very few people would have bet on South-East Asia becoming a future centre of economic power. The Korean conflict, which had shaken all of East Asia, was not long over. Trouble was already brewing between North and South Vietnam. The communist regimes of China and Russia were also at loggerheads, each supporting their own puppet governments and rebel groups throughout the region. Indonesia, the largest and most populous nation in the region, looked increasingly fragile as well. Most of the population lived at little more than subsistence level. Economic growth was slow, the appetite for foreign investment was very limited. Per capita income on average across the region was no higher than it had been in 1900; higher in Singapore and Malaysia, lower in Vietnam and the Philippines.

In the two decades following 1960, the region was rocked by violence, not just the Vietnam war but the bloodbath in Cambodia that accompanied Khmer Rouge rule, the short sharp conflict between China and Vietnam that left several Vietnamese border towns in ruins, and the coup d'etat that ended the Sukarno regime in Indonesia. The Chinese community which had sustained business activity in most countries during years after the World War II, was often caught in the middle, most notably in Indonesia and Vietnam; but in Malaysia too there were tensions as nationalist *bumiputra* governments sought to establish indigenous control over the economy. Yet, as we noted at the end of the Chapter 7, the signs were not all negative. American military aid to Thailand had begun priming the pump there. Singapore offered a base and safe haven for foreign capital. And then the Japanese returned.

Unlike in 1941, the Japanese came back to South-East Asia peacefully, their ships and planes full of goods to trade and cash to invest.

The Japanese economy had, by the end of the 1970s, reached a turning point. In 1945, Japanese industry had lain in ruins, quite literally. The Sony Corporation, today among the country's largest, was first established in a few rooms in a Tokyo department store half-wrecked by American bombs; it was one of the few buildings in the city centre still standing. What had followed is often referred to as the 'postwar Japanese miracle'. A combination of high skills, good education, low wages and inspired business leadership had turned Japan into the world's second largest economy.

Japanese companies had long since outgrown their domestic markets and were seeking access to world markets. They were having some success in penetrating American and European markets in sectors such as automobiles and consumer electronics. But they needed more. South-East Asia, on the brink of economic growth and industrialisation – and its people culturally much more closely affiliated to Japan than either Americans or Europeans were – offered real promise. So Japanese firms began exporting not just cars and televisions and radios, but everything from heavy machinery and power tools for the new factories the region needed, to beauty products and cosmetics for the wives and daughters of the newly affluent middle class.

However, the Japanese needed more than just markets. Two decades of uninterrupted economic growth had pushed up wages in Japan until they were approaching those of the West. That meant rising production costs, and in turn, lower profitability. Other costs had risen too, notably real estate. And an old problem had resurfaced: Japan needed to import virtually all its natural resources, and this too of course had cost implications. Locating centres of manufacturing in production outside the country made economic sense. Already, thanks to strong American influence in both countries, Japanese businesses had been investing heavily in South Korea and Taiwan (the Americans saw Japanese investment as being a counterweight to Chinese influence – as ever, politics affected economics, and vice versa). Now it was South-East Asia's turn.

At time of writing, the newspapers and financial press are full of talk of 'outsourcing' and 'offshoring', the 'new' phenomenon where businesses in the West are moving production facilities, service centres and the like out of their home countries and out to the Far East. But to think of this as new is a mistake. Japanese companies making everything from cars and tractors to refrigerators and power tools were outsourcing production to South-East Asia 25 years ago. Their decision to do so began a revolution in at least some of the region's economies.

At first, Japanese businessmen had to tread carefully. As noted, all of the region had been occupied by the Japanese military during World War II, and the civilian population, especially the ethnic Chinese, had often been brutally treated. In Thailand the occupation had been a relatively light-handed affair and there were fewer unhappy memories. Unsurprisingly, then, it was to Bangkok that Japanese firms began coming in the early 1980s. They found a fairly stable government – for a change – an economy showing signs of life including a nascent financial sector, and a large pool of labour They built factories, invested capital, created jobs.

Other governments began seeing what was happening. Singapore launched a marketing campaign to attract Japanese businesses, especially Japanese financial institutions. Many of these latter were of course connected to the large Japanese industrial groups, the *zaibatsu*, and so could help to fashion networks of relationships with other Japanese companies. Malaysia, already experimenting with economic planning, in 1980 launched its 'Look East' policy. Business owners and managers were encouraged to adopt Japan and Korea as economic role models, and to learn from their management methods and practices. Malaysian businesses should seek both to emulate and to cooperate with Japanese companies. Again, there was a political dimension: the Malaysian government of Prime Minister Mahathir bin Mohamad was looking for a countervailing influence against the dominance of the ethnic Chinese in the Malaysian economy, and the 'Look East' policy was intended to strengthen the hands of the *bumiputra* entrepreneurs.

And, as in South Korea and Taiwan, they showed that the new generation of Japanese business leader could and did possess a great deal of cultural sensitivity. One area where the Japanese excelled was in cultivating relations with local businesses. They showed themselves willing to work with local managers, and even, where necessary, subordinate themselves to them. Malaysia had originally had a rule which insisted that all managerial positions in foreign subsidiaries had to be staffed by Malaysian nationals. Japanese managers were only allowed to serve as 'shadow managers', nominal deputies to the Malays. In fact, in most cases the system worked well and all parties co-operated. Later in the 1980s this system was scrapped and the Malaysian government allowed Japanese to take senior management posts in their own companies. Clearly, they felt that Malaysians were confident and comfortable enough working with Japanese managers for this not to be a problem.

No such problems existed in Thailand, where Japanese companies invested freely, not only in outsourcing manufacturing but also in the country's rapidly growing agriculture and fishing industries. The rich plains of lowland Thailand and the equally rich waters of the sheltered Gulf of Thailand meant that the country had long been a net exporter of food. Japanese companies were eager customers, and Thai agrobusiness expanded rapidly in the 1980s. Leading the way was Charoen Pokphand, the family-owned firm introduced in the previous chapter. Originally established as an agricultural business in 1939, the firm had survived World War II with difficulty. The 1950s had seen a recovery and slow expansion with the setting up of an animal feed mill. In 1963, one of the family, the 24-year-old Chinese/Thai Dhanin Chearavanont, fresh from education in Hong Kong, was appointed managing director. With the support of Bangkok Bank, he expanded the firm's farming activities and also moved into commercial fishing.

In the early 1980s Chearavanont bought the franchise for the 7-Eleven chain of convenience stores in Thailand, and used this profitable venture to build a base in retailing. By 1990 his company, now called CP Group, had diversified into energy, oil and gas, telecommunications and manufacturing, and was also investing heavily in China. CP Group had become South-East Asia's first truly multinational business; by 1997 the group consisted of more than 250 companies in Thailand, Hong Kong and China, and its net worth was estimated at $5.5 billion.

Where Singapore and Thailand led, Malaysia and, a little more hesitantly, Indonesia, followed. Indonesia has always had a history of uneven development, hardly surprising in a nation of 200 million spread over hundred islands and with a cultural diversity ranging from the modern cities of Java to the Stone Age peoples of Irian Jaya. Japanese investment in Indonesia never reached the same levels as in Malaysia or Thailand, but American influence, especially in the 1960s, was stronger. American aid and money helped Indonesia undertake its first attempts at economic planning, and encouraged a liberal business policy. Through the 1970s and 1980s Indonesia remained dominated by small firms. Even by 1990, fewer than 1% of Indonesian businesses could be classified as large (the average for developed economies at the time was nearer 5%). Amid the diffused and fragmented economy of Indonesia, however, one thing stood out. Such few large businesses as existed were almost entirely controlled by Chinese entrepreneurs. It was estimated in 1989 that the Chinese, who comprised 3% of the population of Indonesia, controlled between 60% and 70% of its economy. Pre-eminent among them was Liem Sioe Liong, who had arrived in Java as a refugee from the chaos of postwar China and started a small coffee business. His Salim Group came to be worth an estimated $10 billion.

By the later part of the 1980s, fuelled by investment not only from Japan but also from Europe and North America, and of course, Chinese entrepreneurs from Taiwan and Hong Kong, some of the South-East Asian economies grew rapidly. Cities like Bangkok, Kuala Lumpur and, of course, Singapore, were transformed. And South-East Asia produced businesses of remarkable wealth and power, capable of dealing on equal terms not only with both the big Chinese and Western businesses in Hong Kong such as Wharf International, Hutchison Whampoa, Jardine Matheson and the Swire Group, but also with the big Taiwanese consortia, the Japanese *zaibatsu* and the Korean *chaebol*. Men like Dhanin Chearavanont and Liem Sioe Liong and others – Robert Kwok of the Malaysia/Singapore-based Kerry Group is another excellent example – became among the most widely talked about business leaders in the world.

Thailand and Indonesia were enjoying double-digit annual economic growth by 1990, and Singapore and Malaysia were not far behind. Their economies were transformed in just a few years, from an agriculture and resource extraction to manufacturing for exports. By 1994, 80% of Thailand's gross domestic product was derived from export of manufactured goods. Other parts of the region continued to languish, however. The Philippines remained in turmoil, Burma was sliding deeper into isolation and repression, and Cambodia and Laos remained impoverished, still trying to deal with the aftermath of the recent wars. Vietnam was showing signs of life, and the announcement in 1986 of the policy of *doi moi*, meaning literally 'renovation' or 'rebirth', began creating more favourable conditions for foreign investment. Late to the party, Vietnam also had an additional handicap in the form of its poor political relations with China. The communist government in Hanoi had been backed by the USSR, not China, and had sometimes been seen as Russia's puppet in the region. The 1979 border war between Vietnam and China, and Hanoi's expulsion of the so-called 'boat people', many of them ethnic Chinese rather than Vietnamese, had not improved matters. There were contacts between the Chinese business community in Vietnam and China itself, but these were often small-scale and personal. That fact has continued to hamper Vietnam's growth even today.

By 1990, then, some of the countries of the region were booming, even if others still languished. Western observers began talking about the 'dragon economies', later changing to the 'tiger economies'. The original 'tigers' were Hong Kong, Taiwan, South Korea and Singapore, but by the early 1990s Malaysia and Thailand in particular had also been admitted to the club. It was around this time that the Japanese economic miracle reached its end. Japan's economy began to stall, as a combination of the soaring value of the yen and the consequences of years of economic mismanagement by the Japanese government began to sink in. Japanese investment began to dry up, but by this time, American and European flows were ready to fill the gap. And by this time too, something much more significant had begun to happen.

Earlier, in Chapter 5, we described the economic reform process in China, beginning in the late 1970s, accelerating slowly into the 1980s and beginning to transform the country by the end of the decade. It will be recalled too from earlier chapters that tens of thousands of Chinese fled their native land after the collapse of the empire in 1911 and the ensuing civil war, again during World War II, and yet again in advance of the communist takeover in 1948–9. Many of these settled in South-East Asia. Despite having fled China these refugees and their descendants continued to have ties there; many had left family behind, and had remained in intermittent contact over the years. Some, like the examples mentioned above, had became highly successful, controlling business empires worth billions of dollars.

Partly out of a sense of duty to the ancestral home, but mostly because they scented new business opportunities, the big Chinese-owned businesses of South-East Asia began investing in China. Like their fellows in Hong Kong, they did so with the blessing of the Chinese government, which welcomed their capital and often gave them preferential treatment. CP Group, Kerry Everbright, subsidiaries of the Salim Group and others like them moved into southern and eastern China on a massive scale. They built roads and railways and power stations and other infrastructure projects. They developed property, houses and shopping malls and office blocks; much of the rejuvenated centre of Shanghai, along the Nanjing Road, was built with money raised from South-East Asian investors. CP, with its traditional emphasis on food products, invested heavily in both food production and retail chains. Kerry Everbright built office blocks and hotels.

The Overseas Chinese participated in other ways, too. Large firms, but many smaller ones too, with family or other contacts inside China found there was a demand for a very traditional role, that of middleman. Adventurous Western companies seeking to invest or find markets inside China often lacked knowledge of the country and the language, and also needed contacts. They turned to the Chinese business community in South-East Asia for help and guidance. Sometimes, Western and Overseas Chinese firms formed joint ventures to invest in China together. On other occasions, the latter provided introductions and guidance, for a fee.

At the individual level, young entrepreneurial Overseas Chinese returned to China to start their own businesses, or work as managers for the new Chinese firms springing up in and around Special Enterprise Zones. The latter were often in great demand thanks to their experience of working and managing in free markets and their knowledge of Western ways of doing business. At the same time, they sometimes encountered prejudice and resentment. Some conservative mainland Chinese regarded the 'sojourners' as being second-class citizens for having left the homeland. More important was the fact the Chinese from Hong Kong, Singapore, Malaysia and Thailand could and did command higher salaries than their local counterparts. The big Overseas Chinese investors were resented too, especially when they were given preferential terms or were invited privately to tender for big contracts which were not on public offer. Local businessmen felt they should receive the same treatment. But although there was grumbling, there was rarely little more than that. On the whole, the overseas and mainland Chinese worked harmoniously together. After all, if the mainland Chinese were prepared to welcome back the Japanese, who had devastated their country in World War II, they could certainly do the same for their overseas cousins.

Overseas Chinese investment was probably the single most important factor in China's transformation over the past 20 years. Britain, the USA, Germany and other Western countries have invested heavily; so did Japan. Yet their investments were a drop in the bucket compared to those of the Chinese of Nanyang. By 1995, Britain, the largest foreign investor nation in China, had sent six billion dollars worth of foreign investment into the country. The 60 million Overseas Chinese, including those of Hong Kong, had invested $150 billion. That equates to a contribution of $2,500 from every single Chinese man, woman and child living outside the country; and to a contribution of $120 per head to every man, woman and child living *inside* the country.

In the middle 1990s, World Bank figures suggested that if those 60 million Overseas Chinese had been living together in a single country of their own, that country would have a gross domestic product (GDP) equal to many European nations and nearly two-thirds that of Japan.

In just a few years, the Chinese of Nanyang had become an economic powerhouse. The economic growth rates of countries like Thailand and Indonesia in particular continued in two figures. Western investors, at a time of widespread excess liquidity, continued to pour in money. They recognised that there were risks associated with such high growth, but the rates of return exercised a kind of fascination. As late as 1996, when the cracks were going to appear, a group of leading American investment bankers held a debate on the news channel CNN, arguing over which country offered the best potential for growth. Thailand, said one; no, Malaysia was more stable, said another. Vietnam was more backward, but the *doi moi* policy meant that the country offered immense potential, said a third. Some bankers were still arguing in this vein when the crash came.

The series of events which later came to be known as the Asian crisis began in Thailand. Rapid growth had led to a major expansion of the banking system, which by 1996 included 15 banks and over 100 finance companies. Lending had spiralled out of control; the central bank was unable to exercise sufficient scrutiny. Rapid price inflation meant that assets were over-valued; in the six years from 1987, the Bangkok stock market had increased its capitalisation by 2,400%. Then, in 1996, the Japanese economy took another downturn, and Thai exports to Japan, a key ingredient in economic growth, declined. Borrowers began to have trouble paying back their loans. A major Thai bank failed, amid much publicity. Foreign investment suddenly began to decline as the more canny investors began to get nervous. The Thai currency, the baht, had been pegged to the dollar, and the World Bank and international financial institutions now put pressure on the Thai government to let the baht float freely. That pressure was resisted, but now the whole financial system was under strain. Sixteen bankrupt finance companies were closed down by government order, with no protection for foreign creditors. Now the capital flight began in earnest. The desperate Thai government agreed to let the baht float on 2 July 1997, first closing another 42 bankrupt or ailing finance companies.

But the baht did not float; its value sank like a stone, from its pegged level at 25 to the US dollar to, at one point, more than 50 to the dollar. In 1998, gross domestic product fell by nearly 9%. The Thai government struggled with a set of chaotic bankruptcy laws that seemed to provide little if any protection to any creditor, foreign or domestic. Although Thailand had been fortunate to escape colonial domination, at least some colonies, like next-door Malaysia, had inherited a modern legal and administrative system. Independent Thailand's system had been created through ad hoc borrowings from the US and its own neighbours. As one observer said, the Thai bankruptcy laws and the financial system in general were characterised by uncertainty, lack of trust and lack of leadership.

And of course the effects were not limited to Thailand. In Malaysia, the stock market fell sharply and foreign investment dried up. As reliant on investment capital as Thailand had been, Malaysia had a fundamentally sounder economy and stronger legal/financial system. Growth collapsed from 8% in 1996 to around 2% in 1998, but at least remained positive. Indonesia, on the other hand, teetered on the brink of chaos. The currency, the rupiah, suffered even more heavily than that of Thailand, at one point losing more than 80% of its value. Business bankruptcies were widespread, and 16 banks collapsed. The *pribumi* middle classes were hard hit, many losing their savings. Social unrest broke out, there were riots and attacks on Chinese businesses and homes. The Suharto government's 'New Order' had failed, and the government itself collapsed.

Vietnam, still in the early stages of reform, also suffered; foreign capital had been entering the country tentatively in the years before the crisis, but now foreign investors pulled out in droves, unwilling to face further risk. The Philippines suffered likewise. Being less developed than the other three and less reliant on manufacturing, the overall economic impact was not so great, but economic reform and growth still took a severe knock.

Singapore, as might be expected, came through relatively unscathed. The stock market declined and growth slowed, but the currency was relatively unaffected. Some Western companies did indeed see Singapore as a safe haven, and moved assets and resources there, at least until the dust should settle. Singporean companies often had networks of investment of their own throughout the region, and these suffered financial losses in the places of heaviest exposure, especially Thailand and Indonesia. Perhaps the worst damage of all was done to the region's reputation. Whereas in 1996 South-East Asia had been seen as a good place to invest, now the entire region seemed to have a black mark over it. In reality, it was the structural failings in just a few countries, notably Indonesia and Thailand, that had led to the collapse. The idea of 'contagion', the fear that other markets will be effected like a spreading epidemic and will suffer the same fate, did the rest.

In fact, the recovery from the crisis was relatively swift. In Thailand, after initial confusion, the government called in foreign advisors from banks and consulting firms to help restructure the finance industry and restore trust and credibility. Indonesia did the same. The IMF negotiated financial rescue plans for both countries and also provided support for the Philippines and Vietnam. The Japanese government announced its own rescue package, the Miyazawa Plan, which was to provide $30 billion dollars in aid; however, nothing much ever came of this. Malaysia, which had been building closer links with Japan for some time, did receive $80 million from a consortium of Japanese businesses.

The real saviour, however, was China. While the Japanese market for exports declined, the Chinese market grew. Those South-East Asian manufacturers that remained solvent could still export their way out of trouble by selling into China, and the opportunities for investment and development there remained high. One danger remained, that the Chinese government would succumb to international pressure and let the yuan float. During the crisis years of 1997–8, the yuan would almost certainly have been devalued had it done so. This would have reduced the incomes of exporters into the country, and most certainly have had a further devastating effect on South-East Asia. Fortunately, the international community recognised the danger. Within 12 months, the heads of the IMF and World Bank reversed their positions, from demanding that Beijing let the yuan float, to begging the Chinese government to keep its currency pegged to the dollar.

By 2000, most of the economies most affected by the crisis were growing once more, but more slowly. A new mood of realism seemed to prevail in the region. Since then, governments began seeking more modest growth targets, and looking more at sustainable growth. Malaysia continues its ties with Japan, and may at last be rewarded as the Japanese economy shows signs of life. Growth has been steady if unspectacular in Thailand, Indonesia, the Philippines and Vietnam, and Singapore continues to consolidate its position as the regional financial capital. The post-2000 boom in outsourcing, described above, encompasses companies in many sectors all around the world. Many countries in South-East Asia have benefitted, with Western companies locating manufacturing facilities here to take advantage of good skill levels and lower costs of labour and property. Countries where English is widely spoken, especially the Philippines, have also become favoured destinations for call centres and service centres, competing on a limited basis with India for these kinds of services. While Burma continues in isolation under military rule and Laos remains impoverished, there are signs of hope at last in Cambodia with the discovery of significant deposits of oil in offshore waters.

Crises have continued to rumble through the region. Since 2001 there has been a steady increase in terrorism based on fundamentalist, militant

Islamic movements in Indonesia, southern Thailand and the Philippines. The tsunami at the end of 2005 took hundreds of thousands of lives, but the long-term economic impact has not been so great as feared; already impoverished northern Sumatra remains devastated, the ancient and rich port of Aceh a shadow of its former self. But the tourist resorts of Thailand in particular have recovered quickly. More damaging has been the continued political instability of the country. Yet another military coup d'etat drove the civilian government from office late in 2006, and although the government had been increasingly unpopular and the coup was bloodless, uncertainty and fears of return to the old days caused economic shocks; the stock market and currency both declined again. The threat from the virus H5N1, commonly known as bird flu, also continues to hang over the region. At time of writing, although H5N1 had killed a number of people in Thailand and Indonesia, it had not yet mutated into a strain capable of easy transmission from human to human. Should it do so and a major epidemic result, South-East Asia can expect at the very least a quarantine which will curtail exports and disrupt global supply chains.

One thing that the crash of 1997 made absolutely clear, however, is the regional dominance of China. In the run up to the crisis, it was felt in many quarters that the real economic powerhouse lay in South-East Asia, especially among the Overseas Chinese community. These had, as described above, contributed hugely to the development of China under the auspices of Beijing's economic reform programme. That reform would certainly not have happened as quickly as it did without Overseas Chinese support. But much had changed in the course of 15 years. The crash exposed how fragile the rapidly growing South-East Asian economies really were, and how ill-prepared business leaders and governments were. China, on the other hand, not only weathered the storm but provided long-term economic salvation, and Beijing knew it. Increasingly, from 1998 onward, China began to make its voice heard in the economic and political councils of the region such as ASEAN (Association of South-East Asian Nations). South-East Asian investment and exports are still welcome in China, but the region has lost much of its economic clout. As we shall see in Chapter 11, this poses both dangers and opportunities for South-East Asia. Before we come to consider these, however, we shall look first at the business cultures of South-East Asia, and then at how foreign companies, especially Western companies, work and manage there.

9
Confucius Abroad: South-East Asian Businesses and Managers

To speak of 'businesses in South-East Asia' as though they were a single unified phenomenon is to do the subject less than justice. Just as elsewhere in the world, there is a great deal of diversity. 'Business' can be anything from small corner shops to diversified multinational corporations like CP and Kerry Group, everything from agrobusinesses to specialist high-tech design agencies. It is thus very difficult to generalise about South-East Asian businesses. Equally it is hard to generalise about their managers, who range from old-fashioned entrepreneurs who run their businesses according to time-honoured methods, to modern 'global managers' who have been educated at Harvard Business School or INSEAD and can fit well into any setting.

Generalising becomes still more difficult when we consider the cultural differences that exist between the countries of the region. Although Chinese-owned and managed businesses dominate the economies of most of the countries we are discussing, Chinese owners and managers must, as all owners and managers do, adapt to their environment. And that environment changes, from the Buddhist north to the Islamic south, from advanced economies such as Singapore through developing ones such as Vietnam and the Philippines to still backwards economies such as Burma or Cambodia.

Despite these problems, however, it is possible to discern a common business culture that embraces all of South-East Asia. The culture has, unsurprisingly, many features in common with that of China itself. The migrants from China, and their second-, third- and fourth-generation descendants, are of course highly influenced by the culture of their homeland. The northern mainland countries – Burma, Cambodia, Laos, Vietnam, Thailand – are strongly influenced by China also, and the majority of the population of Singapore are ethnic

Chinese. But Indonesia, Malaysia and the Philippines are not fundamentally different from Thailand or Singapore in terms of business culture.

The causes of this similarity are easy to trace. Despite religious and linguistic differences, all the countries of the region share – along with China, Taiwan, Korea and even Japan – a common cultural heritage in a much broader sense. This means that people from all these countries tend to think in much the same way about certain things: the role of the family, the nature of society, personal relationships and, importantly, education. East Asia and South-East Asia share an education system that, until very recently, was largely dominated by the legacy of the philosophy of Confucius, and Confucian values pervade much of society – business and management included. Indeed, until the fall of the Qing dynasty in 1912, the civil service examination in China was based on readings of the works of Confucius and other classical Chinese thinkers, a practice that was sometimes imitated in neighbouring states.

This is important because, as the sociologists tell us, education shapes how we think about and perceive the world. Education gives us mental frameworks. Experts on cross-cultural management are fond of referring to these frameworks by terms such as 'software of the mind', or 'furniture of the mind'. They do not so much determine *what* we think as *how* we think. A software programme may be used to analyse a wide range of different kinds of data, but the analytical process is determined by the design of the software. Where we sit or stand in a room is determined by how the furniture is arranged. In just the same way, how we think about solving problems or making decisions or relating to other people is determined by the education we receive, formally at schools and universities, informally at home and in society generally.

There have been dozens of books and articles written on the business culture of South-East Asia, but all agree on one thing, the importance of a phenomenon known as the 'Chinese family business'. The great majority of the businesses in the region, including some of the very largest, are owned and managed by members of the same family. Others tend to be owned and managed by kinship groups of other sorts: perhaps a group of friends from the same city or rural district will come together to establish a business, or classmates from the same year at university will, upon graduation, pool their ideas and set up a company. The latter case is common in China itself, and can also be found in South-East Asian countries such as Malaysia and Singapore which have a strong university system. There are also government-owned businesses in some countries, primarily Indonesia and Malaysia, where most if not all of the management team are bumiputras rather than ethnic Chinese, but it is clear that the management style of these have been heavily influenced by the Chinese model. Whether the senior members of the firm are part of the same family or of some other group, the same model prevails. We can therefore discuss the Chinese family business with some confidence as the primary business model of South-East Asia.

One of the most commented-upon features of the Chinese family business is the prominent role played by personal relationships. Indeed, it is difficult to over-state the importance of relationships when doing business in the East. The reason why relationships are so important is that they are the primary means of establishing trust, between individuals and between companies and organisations.

It is sometimes said that one of the differences between Western and Eastern society is that in the West, people put their trust in institutions, while in the East, people put their trust in individuals. For example, in the West we have institutions such as the courts and the legal system which we can rely upon for protection. By and large we trust the legal system to be impartial and to see justice done. In America, and to a lesser extent in Europe and other Western societies, relationships are defined by contract. Party A and Party B agree upon mutual responsibilities, and if one of them fails, the other can use the legal system to either compel the contract to be fulfilled or seek compensation. Eastern society, on the other hand, prefers to establish relationships only with people whom one already knows can be trusted. This has the advantage of making it much less likely that either party will default; if they know and trust each other, they will carry out their side of the bargain without legal compulsion. But it has also has the disadvantage that if trust breaks down, there is no apparent means of redress. And also, how do you know who you can trust?

The answer to the second point is that trust is very often founded upon existing relationships. The first and most important of these is the family. Parents and children, uncles and nieces or nephews, brothers and sisters and cousins form a pre-existing network into which every South-East Asian child is born. By the time one is an adult, other relationships have been formed, with friends, classmates, teachers and the like. But the family relationships tend to remain strongest, and are considered most reliable and most durable. Thus family relationships are often the framework on which businesses are built. In an earlier chapter we mentioned the example of Charoen

Pokphand, now CP Group, the Thai-based multinational corporation. Charoen Pokphand's senior management team has always been dominated by members of the same family, cousins and brothers all descended from the original founders. This same pattern is replicated across thousands of South-East Asian businesses, large, medium and small. And while it is a phenomenon associated most often with Chinese businesses, it is often found in businesses owned and run by people of other ethnic groups as well.

The Chinese term *guanxiwang*, meaning 'network of relationships', is particularly important in understanding how Chinese family businesses operate. The internal management is drawn from a network of family members and, secondarily, friends and other associates. But external relationships are handled in the same way. If the business is looking for a partner to invest in a new venture, its managers turn to members of their own network. Even customer relationships are affected; customers who get preferred treatment are those who are members of the network, while strangers sometimes have to settle for second-best. This of course can have its own problems: for example, when government ministers start awarding contracts to businesses run by friends and family members. This is seen as corruption, and sometimes it is, especially when money changes hands. But sometimes, too, from the perspective of the government minister or the person letting the contract, it is a matter of reducing risk. Better to let the contract to someone we know and can trust, rather than to a stranger, no matter how well qualified the latter is: so goes the logic.

It is sometimes said that Chinese family businesses developed this reliance on relationships because of a lack of strong legal institutions in Eastern cultures. This is not strictly speaking true. China, in particular, has a long history of strong legal institutions both under the empire and under the communists. One of the ancient philosophical systems of China was even called Legalism, and advocated that society should be organised by the rule of law, with strict punishments for violation of the social order and failure to obey the will of the ruler. It is customary to talk of China 'developing' a legal system today, whereas what is happening in fact is that China is adjusting and adapting its legal system to bring it more into line with that of the West. Further, with the exception of Thailand, South-East Asia was under colonial rule for many decades. States such as Malaysia continue to use the British legal system to this day. Vietnam, upon gaining its independence under Ho Chi Minh, likewise continued to use the legal system of the French colonial administration, though adapting it to fit the needs of a communist regime.

The reliance on relationships is part of what we referred to above as the software of the mind. People in South-East Asian societies learn from infancy the importance of the family and of family bonds, just as they do in Southern Europe and the Middle East. They learn the importance of other relationships as they grow older. And in their business careers, even in countries like Singapore where the legal system is trustworthy and very strong, sometimes to the point of authoritarianism, people put their trust in individuals rather than institutions, because that is what they have been educated to do. Relationships are one of the cornerstones of the Confucian philosophical system which, as noted, continues to dominate education and the values of society more generally.

A second cornerstone of that system, and one which is very much related to the first, is the concept of honour to one's elders. Western observers sometimes refer to this as 'paternalism'. In the Confucian system, the father is the head of the family, and all others owe him obedience. But, say the Confucians, this is not blind obedience for the sake of it. As we saw above, the most important relationships are those within families, and within families the most important of all is the relationship between parents and children. Every social institution rests on this premise. Without filial obedience, society would become unstable and order would break down. Obedience to the father is as important in Confucian thinking as obedience to the law is in the West.

The concept of 'fathers' and 'children', in Confucian thinking, goes far beyond blood kinship. As we enter adult life, we find ourselves in other relationships where we owe duties to someone older and wiser than ourselves. The early Confucians emphasised that the teacher should be venerated almost like the head of a family, and that pupils owed their teachers duty on account of their wisdom. Citizens also owed this same duty of respect and obedience to high political officials, provincial governors and the like. In a perfectly natural evolution, heads of businesses became seen as father figures to their employees, even those who were simply hired on and were not part of the employer's family.

The other side of the coin is that the 'father' also has a duty of care and a responsibility to the 'children', and this applies whether we are talking of fathers and sons, teachers and pupils, rulers and people, or managers and workers. In the case of the latter, it is seen as right and natural for employers to care for the welfare of their employees, personally as well as professionally. If a worker is having a problem, be it in the workplace or at home, they will often take these problems to their bosses. There are innumerable stories of this happening. One executive recounted being approached on the golf course at the weekend by one of his workers, who wanted to ask his advice about savings and investments. Another answered the door at his home late one night to be met by an upset worker who was having marital problems. Neither executive was particularly happy about being interrupted in this way. The point is that they did not tell their employees to go away. Irritating though it was to them personally, they stopped, concealed their feelings, listened to their workers and gave the advice that was asked for.

This has a tendency to create organisations that are – by modern Western standards at least – somewhat autocratic. The boss is the boss, and their word is obeyed. It is expected that managers will listen to the views of their employees, should the latter choose to express them, but the final responsibility for any decision is that of the person at the top. Chinese employees do not expect to participate in decision-making, nor is there any evidence that they particularly want to do so. At the same time, if something goes wrong, it is the top manager who takes responsibility, and blame; or at least, should do. Buck-passing and making scapegoats out of juniors does happen, but it is considered highly dishonourable and those who do these things will tend to lose face, with their peers as well as their employees.

This applies even if the boss is a woman rather than a man. In some countries, notably Indonesia and Malaysia, women play prominent roles as entrepreneurs. Not all of them rise to the same prominence as Rini Soewandi, appointed CEO of car-maker Astra International, one of Indonesia's largest companies, in 1998, but it is not uncommon to find women in the boardrooms of large and medium-sized companies in both countries. Nor is there the belief, commonly expressed in the West, that women somehow have different style of management, or different priorities or values. Senior women managers in Chinese family businesses have the same Confucian mindset and the same values, and manage in the same way, as the men. It follows that they are just as hard-nosed and just as autocratic as the men, too.

The third cornerstone of the Chinese family business is a sense of community and belonging, sometimes known as collectivism. In the West we tend to think a great deal in terms of self. The ego plays a very important role in our thinking, about ourselves and about other people. In Chinese and South-East Asian societies, however, the community plays a much more important part. The interests of the community, it is held, should come before the interests of self. In practice this does not always happen, of course, but it should be noted that much more social pressure is put on people who are held to be selfish, to stop being so and consider the interests of the community. Self-interest is not held to be a virtue, be it enlightened or otherwise. The most important community in these societies is, of course, the family, but there are other communities too: village, tribe, ethnic group, professional associations, university cohorts and the like. Employees of a business are likely to feel that same sense of community. And when, as very often happens, the business is owned and managed by a family, the ties become doubly strong.

These collectivist organisations tend to be much less formal than their counterparts in the West. People have roles as part of the family, or at least, a family-style network. Therefore there is less need for formal hierarchy; everyone already knows their roles and what is expected of them. Unfortunately, this informality often also extends to matters such as record keeping. Minutes of vital meetings are not always kept; instead, people will rely on their collective memory of what happened last time. Performance of individual workers and managers is measured informally, if at all. Financial record-keeping can also be haphazard, as banks and foreign investors learned to their cost during the Asian crisis of 1997–8. Another problem arises around the issue of loyalty. Employers and managers are expected to be loyal to the firm, just as they would to a family. This tends to discourage whistle-blowing; anyone who spots sharp practice by a senior manager and reports it to the authorities will surely be ostracised by their colleagues. Even leaving a job to go and work for a rival or start one's own business can be seen as disloyal, and such departures have to be negotiated carefully.

From the above, it can be seen that Chinese family businesses possess some very decided strengths, but also have their weaknesses. Among the strong points is flexibility. Without formal hierarchies and organisation structures to worry about, these businesses tend to be very flexible. Time and time again, we see them moving very rapidly to take advantage of new business opportunities. Despite the remarks on record-keeping, prudent financial management is highly valued. Businesses tend to accumulate cash savings, and even though the financial systems of the region have become more sophisticated, there is a still a preference for funding growth through cash rather than bank loans, which are seen by many as second-best. Among more conservative people especially, there is real suspicion of those who incur heavy debt.

The family model also tends to reject public ownership. Owners of growing companies will sometimes sell off part of their company through the stock market to raise capital, but they will usually retain majority control in their own hands. The separation of ownership and control, regarded as one of the strengths of the Western management system, is viewed with suspicion by many Chinese. Give away ownership, it is reasoned, and you give away control as well.

These businesses, then, tend to be very flexible and adaptable. However, they also have their fragilities. With so much depending on the bonds of trust and loyalty, there is the risk that if something damages or breaks those bonds, the business will collapse. Much depends on the leader. He or she has to be capable of inspiring trust and making decisions, to have a strong will and a good business brain. One fundamental weakness of the family model is that when the founding leader dies or retires, there must be other family members ready and able to step into place. Business termination rates – that is, the number of businesses that are sold or closed down are higher in South-East Asia than in most parts of the world, and this problem of succession is a principal cause of this. In some cases, the founding leader hands control to another family member who is not capable of managing the business. In others, if no family member can be found to take over, the owner will sell the business or even close it down entirely. Of course this happens in other parts of the world too, but the problem is more common in South-East Asia, and helps to explain why few businesses, even big ones, last for more than a few generations; some do not even last that long.

Because so much responsibility and authority rest on the leader, he or she has to be very capable indeed. Collective leadership or shared leadership is not widely found. Among the many things for which the leader is largely, sometimes even solely, responsible is strategy. It is the leader who determines the business's goals, and how it will reach them. Once the decision is made, it is communicated to everyone else in the business, and each manager and employee is expected to support the decision loyally and do their part.

Strategic planning, like so much else, tends to be informal. Whereas Western corporations often have planning departments and issue formal structured plans, such things are rare in the Chinese family business. If there is a strategic plan, it is probably a few sheets of paper in the senior manager's desk; more likely, it is carried in his or her head. Rather than structured plans, Chinese businesses favour what modern theorists call 'emergent' strategy. That is, instead of laying out a series of steps and a timetable towards goals, Chinese businesses tend to have a much more unstructured approach. Although the goal is important, the means to getting there are less so. This leaves the manager and the business free to react to new threats, and take advantage of new opportunities as they arise, rather than being constrained by formal plans.

While Western thinking on strategy has been dominated over the last few decades at least by the strategic models developed by theorists such as Igor Ansoff and Michael Porter, Chinese strategic thinking tends to reach further back into Asian culture. The *Art of War*, written by the general Sunzi (Sun Tzu) in the 6th century BC and heavily revised in the 3rd century AD, remains a source of inspiration. So does another ancient Chinese text, *The Thirty-Six Strategems*, which offers a series of precepts to be followed. Both works, and others like them, tend to concentrate on those things which must be done to ensure victory: the requisites for a successful strategy, rather than generic strategies of the type favoured in the West. Ancient Chinese texts on strategy emphasised the need to gather information in advance of action, to prepare thoroughly, to be patient and wait for opportunity, to use deception whenever possible to confuse the enemy and put him off guard, and then when the opportunity does come, to move swiftly and decisively. Not surprisingly, observers today report that Chinese managers, when thinking about strategy, tend to favour qualitative information over quantitative, to spend a great deal of time thinking and processing information before acting, and then to be much swifter at making decisions and acting than are their Western counterparts. The average Chinese manager probably does not have a copy of the *Art of War* on his or her desk (though a surprising number do), but the software of the mind has conditioned him or her to think in this way nonetheless.

When we turn to other aspects of management we find the picture looks similar. Personnel management or human resource management is a big part of the Western style of management, and every business of any size has an HR department. This concept is quite foreign to the Chinese family business; even today, even among large businesses, few have formal HR departments, and where these do exist they are small and lacking in influence. Managing people is considered to be one of the jobs of the leader. The leader can no more delegate responsibility for managing his or her staff than the father of a family can delegate responsibility for his children.

This is not to say that the course of personnel management and industrial relations always runs smoothly in Chinese family businesses.

These have their fair share of disputes and labour problems. It can be argued that the lack of a professional HR department makes the problem worse; senior managers in some cases lack the training and experience necessary to manage people effectively. After all, the first labour management departments – as they were then known – appeared in Western businesses in the early 20th century precisely because of this problem, and the aim of bringing a more disciplined and better balanced approach to the management of people. A century on, and the jury is still out on how effective they have been; HR departments have in some cases become formal and bureaucratic institutions that do not serve the needs of either the company or its workers. Chinese family businesses tend to have the opposite problem, in that a lack of structure coupled with weak leadership can lead to lack of direction, confusion over roles and tasks, and general dissatisfaction. Once again, much depends on the leaders of the business and how well they perform. A strong leader makes for a strong company, and weak leader makes for a weak one.

Turning to marketing, it will come as no surprise by now to learn that South-East Asian businesses rely heavily on personal relationships and networks. This is particularly true in terms of business-to-business marketing. In the late 1980s and early 1990s Western academics began developing a theory of 'relationship marketing', which argued that marketing goals were best achieved by first building a relationship with the customer. This tended to promote a better understanding of the customer's needs, which in turn meant that the selling company could better develop products and services to meet those needs. This in turn strengthened the relationship further, creating a virtuous circle. Repeat business and greater customer loyalty were seen as among the benefits.

By the late 1990s the academics were beginning to realise that Chinese family businesses has been practising relationship marketing for many years. A great deal of study was devoted to the subject, and the general conclusion was that although this type of marketing had some very great strengths, it also had a few weaknesses. It is easier to develop a commercial relationship with people you know and trust, and this happens everywhere; a great deal of relationship marketing is done in the clubhouses of golf courses around the world, for example. As well as trust, there is also a more intimate knowledge of the customer and what they might need. The main difficulty comes when you reach the limits of the network: existing customers are already fully satisfied, and there are no more customers to be marketed to. The options then are to expand the network, which is not easily done, or to form alliances with partners in order to have access to their networks (one reason why joint ventures are so popular among South-East Asian firms). Even today, very few South-East Asian businesses employ formal market research in order to identify new customers and new opportunities.

While personal selling and relationships play a critical role in business-to-business markets, consumer markets require a different approach. It has been often remarked that the consumers of South-East Asia – and of Asia generally – are more brand-conscious than those of the West. They tend to react more strongly to brands, quickly rejecting or accepting new brands. When a new brand is accepted, consumers tend to be more loyal and to identify themselves more closely with the brand than is common in the West. Two riders need to be added: the research on which these findings are based is fairly fragmentary, and there are signs that South-East Asian consumers, in the more developed countries at least, are growing more sophisticated in their approach. But it is probably fair to say that most consumers do stick to the brands they know.

The reason for this, once again, is trust. Trust was identified as one of the key attributes of any brand as long ago as the 1830s, when the mathematician and economist Charles Babbage pointed out that people used a maker's mark or trademark as an assurance of reliability when they could not test product quality for themselves. The Chinese have been using brand marks since the 17th century if not before, so they too are familiar with the concept. In societies characterised by social and political instability, as is true in many South-East Asian countries, people search for things that they can trust, certainties when all else is uncertain. The strong brand consciousness of consumers is thus a product of two things: a natural tendency to see relationships as important, and a need for certainty and trust.

When we look at distinctive brands which have emerged in South-East Asia, as opposed to Western or Japanese or Korean imports, we can see that these features are very prominent. For example, Banyan Tree Hotels, the resort hotel chain with its headquarters in Singapore, makes a very strong feature of comfort and reliability of service (and backs this up with a staff training programme that many Western hotel chains would do well to emulate). Banyan Tree appeals to a global clientele, but it sticks to distinctively South-East Asian identity, reinforcing the fact that it is part of the local culture; this, as well as appealing to customers, also sends a reassuring message to employees and others in the communities where the company operates. On another level, the coffee house chain Trung Nguyen, sometimes called the 'Vietnamese Starbucks' and one of the most successful of the new Vietnamese entrepreneurial ventures, owed its initial success by appealing to customers as a local business, part of their own community, owned by people just like themselves. As Trung Nguyen has expanded, including into other countries such as Canada and Australia, the brand image has had to evolve, but community and trust remain a big part of the brand image. Indeed, these same values also play a prominent role in the Starbucks brand, and values such as trust, community and quality play an important role everywhere. It must be emphasised that the difference here is one of degree rather than kind. It is not that trust is absent from Western brands, but rather that trust is even more important in the East than in the West.

One interesting feature of recent times has been the growth of Western-style management education in South-East Asia. Most universities of any size now have business schools offering both undergraduate and graduate degrees, including MBA degrees. Thousands of young men and women also travel to North America, Europe and Australia to study management at the business schools there. A decade ago, it was widely assumed this would lead to a general breakdown of the Asian business model and that these young managers educated in the Western style would adopt Western methods wholesale. At time of writing, there is little sign of this happening. South-East Asian managers are adapting rather than adopting. They are learning techniques and skills which they are importing into South-East Asia, and are certainly becoming much professional in areas such as financial management or the management of intellectual property. But there is little if any evidence to suggest that the basic family model is changing, or will change in the near future. Relationships and trust still count for more than contracts and law.

At the beginning of this chapter we noted that there are variances within and between countries, and that these can make it difficult to generalise about South-East Asian business culture. This chapter concludes with a look at individual countries and comments on some of the variances that can be expected.

With regard to Burma, Laos and Cambodia, there is relatively little to say. Burma's military dictatorship has, as noted, allowed little in the way of economic development. Its few large business entities are mostly under direct or indirect state control. Within that context, one might expect to find Burmese managerial culture conforming very much to the relationship model described above. With fewer Western influences to contend with, and operating under difficult conditions – to say the least – Burmese businesses have been forced into an even stronger dependence on personal relationships and networks. The same applies in Laos and Cambodia, although for different reasons. The lack of a strong government and strong economy has in both countries forced people back into dependence on personal networks. Again, we can expect the relationship model to be very strong.

Vietnam is an intriguing case. Vietnamese management culture had begun to modernise in the mid-1990s, before the Asian crisis caused a temporary setback. Even into the early years of the 2000s, Vietnam suffered from a lack of skilled managerial talent. Those few managers with training or experience, especially from the ethnic Chinese community, often went abroad to seek their fortunes. But more recently, as the example of Trung Nguyen shows, a class of successful Vietnamese entrepreneurs has begun to emerge. Vietnam's business culture is very similar to that of China, and the family model described here prevails among both Vietnamese and Chinese. One welcome development is the improvement of relations between the two communities, after the tensions that followed the end of the Vietnam War in 1975, when many thousands of Chinese fled overseas. Now, especially in Ho Chi Minh City, where the Chinese community is concentrated, there is a good deal of cooperation, and it seems likely that Vietnamese entrepreneurs are learning from their Chinese neighbours. This, plus the physical proximity of China, suggests that the Chinese model will remain strong.

The same is true of Thailand, a much more advanced country economically, though not without its troubles as we have noted in earlier chapters. The Chinese and Thai communities have become very much mingled together, and each has influenced the other. Studies of ethnic Thai businesses and managers have shown that if anything, Thais are even more devoted to the relationship model, and to value such things as paternalism and collectivism even more highly, than the Chinese. Key values in Thai business culture include *sia khwam ru suek* (avoidance of criticism) and *raksa nam jai* (polite personality). Maintaining good relationships is seen as of paramount importance. Thai managers will go to extreme lengths to avoid hurting the feelings of others or telling them unpleasant news.

One minor but important difference which observers have noted lies in the importance of the individual. Another Thai concept, *alum aluay*, translates roughly as 'person over system', implies that although the individual owes a duty to the family or other social unit just as in the

Chinese model, the family also owes a strong duty of care to the individual. Face is probably more important in Thai culture than anywhere else in the region, and causing another member of your social group to lose face is a serious offence. In terms of business culture this means that people tend to look out for each others' interests, and in times of crisis, ranks are closed against outsiders.

Perhaps under the influence of Theravada Buddhism, Thai culture tends to stress the mystical and the spiritual. Karma plays an important role, and there is a strong element of fatalism. People tend to make personal judgements based on spiritual as well as physical and mental qualities. One of the most important qualities a leader can have is *baramee*, a term with no exact English translation but whose approximate meaning is 'charismatic and well-loved'. Another important quality is *khunatham*, meaning kindness or compassion. Skill, decisiveness – and indeed, integrity – come much lower down on the list. The relationship in Thailand, even more than elsewhere in the region, means everything; without relationships, nothing is possible.

The Philippines also has some unusual features. The American colonial regime left a strong legal system, and as a result, Filipinos probably have more interest in and respect for contract law than elsewhere in the region. Another American heritage is the value placed on formal education, including formal management education. Filipinos have been travelling abroad, mostly to the USA, to take formal management training since the 1960s, long before people from other countries of the region. Many of these people, who included in their number many ethnic Chinese, then found work elsewhere in the region, especially in Malaysia and Singapore, where their skills and training gave them more opportunities than at home. In the 1990s, as the Filipino economy revived, some of these managers, who now had international experience and networks, returned home to help in the revival. Although there are wide variations in terms of education, training and talent in the Filipino management pool, top Filipino managers are sophisticated experts in the art of modern management.

That aside, the business culture of the Philippines looks much like the culture described above. Ethnic Filipinos value relationships as much as do the Chinese. Ironically, the importance of relationships was established during the long period of Spanish colonial rule, when most of the country was divided up into landed estates in a quasi-feudal manner, and landowners encouraged their tenants to be loyal to themselves personally rather than to the colonial power. And again, there has been influence from the Chinese business community.

Despite some rough patches in the past, relationships between the two communities are good, and intermarriage is also very common.

Indonesia is perhaps the most complex management culture to describe, in part because of the very ethnically diverse nature of Indonesian society. The policy of *bhineka tunggal ika*, 'unity in diversity', which critics have regarded as a cover for an attempt to stamp out ethnic differences and 'Javanise' the entire archipelago, has been only partly successful. However, Indonesian business culture does have many common features. Chief among these are a strong reliance on personal networks and relationships, and a strongly paternalistic culture. The *bapak* (father) and *ibu* (mother) are highly important figures in Indonesian society, and it is not uncommon for these terms to be used outside the family. The boss, for example, will be called *bapak*. Indonesian academics have even coined a term, *bapakism*, which means roughly 'vertical orientation', or in plain language, the tendency for everyone to look up to the leader.

Indonesian ideas on leadership are not unlike those found elsewhere in the region, but there are some interesting variations. One idea sometimes found in writing on the subject is the threefold concept of leadership: (1) leadership by example, (2) leadership by encouraging others and (3) giving direction, or leading in the right direction. This is sometimes described as, respectively, leading from the front, leading from the middle and leading from behind. It is important to note that these are not choices; a good leader is seen as someone who does all three simultaneously. As in Thailand, the bond with the leader is highly personal; as in Thailand too, Indonesian business culture seeks to avoid confrontation and loss of face. Losing one's temper or showing anger before colleagues is likely to cause in loss of face for oneself.

Malaysia too has its cultural differences, in part because the Chinese population is much larger and is more heavily represented in the general workforce. When Chinese and Malays work alongside each other in the same business, relations are generally very good, but managers have to take care as it is easy for tensions to build up. Seemingly little things can often cause problems. It is, for example, necessary to have two canteens: Chinese workers prefer to eat pork, while the Muslim Malays are prohibited from doing so. During the traditional Malay holiday of Hari Raya, many bumiputras will take anything up to a week off work in order to return to their home villages to celebrate with their families. One factory thought it had found a clever way of using this to advantage by timing its factory shutdown for maintenance to coincide with the festival week. However, all the staff employed on the maintenance programme had to be Chinese, as there were no Malay workers available. Learning of this, the Malay workers thought that they were being squeezed out of the engineering department and lodged a grievance with their union. The problem was only settled after some fairly tricky negotiations.

Malaysia, like Singapore, inherited the British legal and educational systems, which have been maintained very well. Malaysians have some of the highest standards of education in South-East Asia. Malaysians are also more likely to put their trust in contract law than are any of their neighbours, and seem comfortable working in Western legal and administrative frameworks. Yet, kinship ties remain very powerful, and paternalism and collectivism are strong values. Yet Malaysians also remain very spiritual people, and even the most modern and high-tech factories have their red 'spirit houses' to which offerings must be made on a regular basis to keep the spirits happy. In Malaysia, the modern and the traditional co-exist, often in very close proximity to each other.

Singapore has been deliberately left to last, for it is the most advanced economy of the region and the one where Western managers are most likely to feel at home. Over the years, Singapore has learned a great deal from both Western and Japanese ways of doing business. But the learning, as we have said above, has taken the form of adaptation to local needs, not wholesale adoption. Despite its excellent universities with their Western-style business schools, despite its very strong legal system, Singapore remains at heart a Chinese city with Malaysian and Indian overtones. Confucian values dominate thinking and education. Relationships, paternalism and collectivism are the cornerstones of the business culture, even in the most modern and advanced businesses. What is more, the Singaporeans seem to have worked out how to translate their adherence to traditional Chinese values into a virtue and a source of advantage. Instead of falling back on relationships as the one certain source of trust in an uncertain world, they build on and leverage their relationships to achieve business growth and expand their horizons.

Taken in sum, then, with some regional variances and exceptions, the 'Chinese family business' remains the most common model of business found in South-East Asia. There are no signs that this is going to change soon. This model is not without its weaknesses, but it strengths are very real. Well-managed Chinese family businesses are formidable competitors, as recent history has shown. The business culture which emphasises trust, relationships and harmony is strikingly at odds with the more abrasive and competitive cultures of the West, especially America. How Western managers work in this environment and how they build their own relationships with Chinese and other local partners is the subject of the next chapter.

10 Seven Paths to Happiness: Doing Business in South-East Asia

Western businesspeople travelling to South-East Asia or preparing to work with South-East Asian business partners for the first time often make one of two mistakes. The first is to assume that the business culture they are entering will be just like their own, and the same rules, methods, procedures and ways of doing things will apply. The second is to assume the opposite, that the business culture they are entering is entirely alien and foreign, and nothing will look remotely familiar.

The truth, as is so often the case, lies somewhere in between. There are similarities; there are also some very strong differences. South-East Asian business owners and managers want the same basic things as their counterparts in the West. They want to run successful businesses that make a profit. They seek growth and expansion and innovation. On a personal level, they want to make good money, have comfortable lives and provide well for their families. Indeed, realising that common interest is an important first step in doing business anywhere in the region. Before we go on to talk about cultural differences, it should be stressed that Western people should not be too deferential to local culture. The Westerner who tries to imitate local habits and customs in every respect will likely be looked on with either amusement or contempt, depending on how badly he or she gets things wrong. It is important, especially when going to the region for the first time, to 'be yourself'. Many people, especially educated, well-off people in South-East Asia admire Western culture, and Western business methods. They will be as interested in learning from you as you are in learning from them. The strength of any business deal will depend not on how 'Eastern' you can be, or how 'Western' your partners are prepared to be, but on how well you manage to bring the best characteristics of East and West together.

For although Western and South-East Asian managers and business owners will generally want the same things, the methods by which they go about getting them will differ. As we noted in the previous chapter, the philosophy of Confucius has had a pervasive effect on the education systems of every country in the region. There have also been religious overlays, of Buddhism in the north, Islam in the south, Christianity in pockets here and there, and there are also variations according to national culture and, especially in Indonesia and the Philippines, regions within each country. All of these things have a pervasive effect on business culture. Equally important for the Western manager, however, is to remember that he or she too is a product of their own culture. Our own education has equally shaped our own thinking. We are products of a system of education that goes back to classical times; as the philosopher and mathematician Alfred North Whitehead once said, all of us in the West are the products of Aristotle. There have been other influences too; the rationalism of Descartes, our own religious traditions both Catholic and Protestant, the humanism of the Enlightenment, the tradition of scientific thinking pioneered by Darwin and Kelvin. All of these influences and many others have helped to shape our thinking, usually so subtly that we are not really aware of it.

The point is that when a Western manager goes to South-East Asia – and, of course, vice versa – it is necessary to remember that expectations, patterns of thinking will be different. People may make decisions in different ways. As we pointed out in Chapter 6, negotiating styles will differ. Customers will have different perceptions and ideas about products. Employees have different relationships with their bosses and with the companies that employ them. Managers do things like making strategy and gathering information in different ways. It is important not to make value judgements about these things – or at least, not to let it show that one is doing so. Neither system is entirely right nor entirely wrong. The Western systems of management and business culture have their failings; so do those of the East. In the West, we manage businesses as we do because it is how we have been trained to do so, and the system even with its imperfections is what we are used to.

It is this ability to think outside the old accepted patterns, that have been instilled in us through education, training and experience, that makes cross-cultural management so difficult. The problems that we experience in every day working life become magnified when we are working with or dealing with people whose culture is unfamiliar to us.

We become uncertain. We can no longer predict so easily what people will do or how they react; we are less able to determine what they want. When business organisations are structured differently to what we are used to, we are not sure who our contacts should be, or even who the leader is. With uncertainty comes risk; when we do not know the situation, we are more likely to make bad decisions.

The only way to solve this problem is to learn, as much as possible, about the cultures and people we are dealing with. Training and experience, once again, can help Western people to become more comfortable and familiar with cultures in places such as South-East Asia. This includes learning about ways of doing business, but also much more. The more we know about a place, the more comfortable we feel in it. Take the example of language training. It is sometimes argued that it is not really necessary to learn foreign languages as English is now widely spoken and has become the *lingua franca* of the business world; everywhere one goes, one will find people who speak English. Strictly speaking, that may be true. But not being able to understand what is being said around you can become a handicap in many situations, professional and social alike. One of the authors recalls being at dinner some years ago with a group of businessmen from Shanghai. One of the waiters, a Cantonese, annoyed the party, who began discussing and criticising him in their own Shanghai dialect. The waiter of course could not understand a word, and had no idea that he was being insulted or even that he had offended anyone. This is a trivial example, but it shows how not knowing a language can cause problems – and how one can remain unaware that a problem has even been caused.

For a Westerner, running a successful business in South-East Asia means being able to understand and adapt one's thinking to local circumstances. An anonymous ancient Chinese poet once wrote a verse in which he identified the seven ways to happiness. Ultimate happiness, he wrote, can be found by paying respect and living in harmony; by gentle behaviour and calmness at all times; by being tolerant of the faults of others but seeking always to correct the faults of oneself; by displaying patience and humility; by having a sincere heart; by seeking tranquility rather than riches; and by accepting the decrees of the heavenly emperor. Today, the paths to happiness are perhaps a little different. With apologies to the poet, here are our own seven paths to, if not happiness, then at least to understanding and knowledge when running a business in South-East Asia.

1 *Relationships and trust are essential*. This is a universally acknowledged truth. Westerners and Chinese and *bumiputras*, businessmen

and academics, anyone with experience of South-East Asia, will repeat this. Entire books have been written on this subject alone. The Chinese concept of *guanxi*, as we noted in Chapter 6, is a cornerstone of business throughout the region. Some have argued that *guanxi* is even more important in South-East Asia than in China itself. The history of political turbulence and violence in many countries means that people tend only to business with those that they know and trust.

Accordingly, South-East Asian business leaders and managers devote a great deal of time to building networks and establishing trust. Western managers will find they need to do the same. In negotiations, for example, it can take weeks, even months of talks before either party finally comes to the point. There is often a great deal of talking around the issues, or discussion of entirely irrelevant points. Westerners sometimes think that their opposite numbers are stalling, or playing for time, or playing some more devious game. Sometimes, of course, they are doing one or more of these things. But very often, they are simply sizing up their opposite numbers and getting to know them better.

The best response is to play along with this, to let oneself be sized – and to use the opportunity to do a little sizing up on one's own. Trust is a reciprocal arrangement, and one should be able to trust one's partners in any event. These negotiations are particularly important because, even in situations where formal contracts are signed, they are effectively valueless without the establishment of trust – as Western companies often find out to their cost. And in some countries and some cases, even a formal contract is very much an optional extra. This is changing, but it is changing slowly.

One common mistake that Western businesspeople make is to go into the first meeting prepared to talk tough and reach a resolution as soon as possible. This will usually receive a very negative reaction. Another mistake is to rely on formal presentations rather than simple conversation. Several years ago, an American consulting company pitching for business to a Chinese-owned firm went into the meeting room with a team of sharp-suited consultants and a Power Point presentation lasting for an hour. The presentation gave a wealth of detail about the consulting firm and its methods, but the Chinese managers soon grew restive. After about ten minutes, they politely asked that the presentation be stopped; they wanted to ask the consultants what exactly was being offered to their business. After a brief discussion, the consultants refused and carried on with the presentation. The Chinese managers sat silently through the remainder, and at the end, again politely, the Americans were shown to the door. One of the Chinese managers said later, 'How could we do business with these people? They will not let us get to know them.'

While it takes time to establish relationships, the rewards for the creation of a successful relationship can be very great. Once trust is there, unless something happens to violate that trust, then partnerships can last for a long time. More, for a Western company or manager, establishing a relationship of trust with a South-East Asian firm is likely to mean that in time, the partner will introduce you to other friends. Thus the *guanxiwang*, the network of relationships, expands, opening new doors and creating new business opportunities. It is for this reason that many Western businesses opt for joint ventures with local firms, especially when first establishing themselves. Joint ventures were once required by law in some countries, such as Vietnam in particular; no Western company could set up a wholly-owned subsidiary, it had to take a local partner. Those rules have now been relaxed, at least in Vietnam, but even so some Western businesses continue to see advantages in the joint venture option. A successful joint venture allows the Western company to learn more quickly about markets and the business environment. It also gives the Western partner access to the local company's networks, which can be good for both sides. Of course, joint ventures are notoriously tricky things to negotiate and manage, and a good many fail, sometimes acrimoniously. The financial press is full of stories of such cases, but these stories should not put anyone off. The press is quick to report failed joint ventures, but it spends much less time reporting on successful ones.

Successful joint ventures are founded on strong relationships and bonds of trust, but the same is true of other business relationships too. In South-East Asia, a company's reputation is a powerful force when it comes to hiring staff. The company does not necessarily have to be large or prestigious, but it does have to have a reputation for caring for its workers. Firms which get a bad reputation in this respect can find key workers leaving, and can also find that they are hard to replace once they have gone. And customers also want to deal with firms they can trust. It is, as we have noted, almost impossible to overstress the importance of relationships when doing business in this region. Relationships are the alpha and the omega, the first and the last, the foundation on which business ventures are built and the channels through which business is done. Learning the art of relationship-building is of primary importance, and should be done before even setting foot in South-East Asia.

2 *Be polite and have good manners.* Politeness is an important virtue in every society in the region. People who have good manners and behave in a dignified way are more likely to gain acceptance and respect. Behaving brusquely, speaking loudly and using vigorous hand gestures can all send negative signals to those you are dealing with. Losing one's temper in public can result in major loss of face. In some countries, even raising one's voice publicly can cause distress to others.

This does not mean that the Chinese and other South-East Asians do not lose their tempers, or that they never argue. They are human, and they do. But these things are seen as much more serious matters than in some parts of the West. South-East Asian peoples do not by and large believe in the Anglo-Saxon need to 'express themselves'. On the contrary, it is seen as right and acceptable to conceal one's true feelings, especially if they would give offence to others.

The Chinese also have a strong, if occasionally somewhat earthy, sense of humour, and enjoy laughter and jokes. So do the other peoples of South-East Asia; the Thais in particular are noted for their love of story-telling and humour. One of the problems of course is that humour sometimes does not travel; a joke that may be very funny to a Singaporean Chinese may be utterly bewildering to an Englishman or an American. A famous story is told of General Douglas MacArthur, the American pro-consul in Japan immediately after the war, who made the mistake of telling a very lengthy and very American joke to an audience of Japanese officials. His translator listened faithfully but in complete incomprehension. When the general had finished the translator, despairing, turned to the audience and said, 'The general has just told a joke. Everyone should now please laugh.' The audience duly did. A Westerner on the receiving end of an incomprehensible Chinese joke might consider following suit; especially in a large group; polite laughter is less likely to give offence than a blank stare.

One important consequence of this is that when a question is asked, the listener will sometimes tell you what you want to hear, not what you need to know. Western market researchers have always found this a problem. When asked their perceptions of a brand and whether they purchased it, respondents would often give highly favourable opinions. This was done so as to avoid hurting the researcher's feelings, especially if he or she worked for the company that produced the brand in question. In order to get around this, it is necessary to use independent researchers and to ask questions that 'talk around' the product and gain general impressions. Direct questions will not necessarily receive faithful answers.

Much has been written too about the need to use correct etiquette, for example, at meals. While good manners need to be observed and one must not give offence, it is important not to worry too much about this. South-East Asian peoples by and large do not expect Westerners to be familiar with their customs. Indeed, instructing or helping a stranger is something that many enjoy. Learning from your hosts can help give the latter more face. On the other hand, those who try slavishly to imitate local customs are often looked upon with suspicion, rather like American tourists who wear kilts on the streets in Scotland. It is much more important, as the ancient poet said, to have a sincere heart. Honesty and integrity will win respect and trust, but they have to be displayed through personal behaviour. As a simple rule of thumb, be polite but friendly, and this should see the visitor through pretty much any situation, personal or professional.

3 Practice tolerance and learn to think like others. As we noted at the outset of this chapter, one of the keys to managing across cultural boundaries is the ability to learn other ways of thinking. Not every Westerner going to South-East Asia will necessarily learn to 'think Confucian' or fully understand the mindset of the people he or she deals with, although we would recommend that some effort be made. But it is essential to recognise that things will be different. There will be obvious differences in things such as appearance, language, food, climate and so on. More difficult to deal with are the subtle, often invisible differences in behaviour, attitude and thought.

Tolerance is of course much easier to talk about than to practise. But one habit of mind that it is useful to cultivate – and this is true in professional as well as personal situations – is to question one's own assumptions about what one hears and sees. To take the example just given, the market researcher who hears a member of the public tells him something which is blatantly untrue might reflect on the other person's motives. Is this person trying to deceive you, or is he/she merely trying to spare your feelings? Similarly, a manager who asks an employee whether a particular task has been carried out, only to find later that it has not, might think the employee was idle or shirking. Equally, it might be that the employee did not want to upset his boss with an unpleasant or negative answer, fearing that this would then upset the harmony of the workplace. In the end, the Western manager will find himself or herself falling back on the personal knowledge of the particular employee in order to determine which motive is more likely, and this brings us back again to the question of relationships.

Customs which might seem unusual, even bizarre in the West are considered perfectly normal in South-East Asia. In the last chapter we mentioned how some Malaysian factories still have 'spirit houses' and managers need to remember to make offerings to placate the spirits. It might seem laughable to us, but entire factories have been shut down, sometimes for days, when the workforce believes that the spirits are angry; in some cases, a holy man has to be brought in to 'cleanse' the factory before staff will return to work. One could get angry and threaten to fire the workers unless they return to work, but one then has to reflect whether frightened and upset workers are really going to be giving of their best. It might be better to go ahead and make offerings to the spirits.

On a more sophisticated level, tolerance is a virtue too in negotiations. South-East Asian negotiators will have their own ways of doing things, their own methods of raising items for discussion and resolving debates. It is tempting for Western managers to try to take over and run things their way. But this kind of assertiveness often does not go down very well. Understanding the needs of the other party and respecting them can win respect in turn. This does not mean the Western negotiator should be passive and let the other side have their own way. It is important to set out one's own position. But the little ceremonies and rituals that often accompany negotiations must be allowed to take place, even if they are time-consuming.

4 Cultivate patience. You will need it. Negotiations and business deals in South-East Asia are sometimes concluded quickly, but more normal practice is for them to drag on for weeks and months. Often, this is the result of the need to build relationships and for the parties to get to know and trust each other. Sometimes, it is a deliberate test. Waiting quietly for the enemy to make the first move and reveal his game is an old Chinese stratagem, employed in war, sport, politics and business alike. Knowing this, and knowing when to wait in turn, can also win respect.

And along with the need for trust, many Chinese businessmen enjoy negotiations for their own sake. 'We could have reached a deal earlier', a Malaysian Chinese businessman once confided to an American, 'but we have enjoyed your company very greatly; we did not want to let you go.' Others may see negotiations as a game, a chance to exercise their wits against another. Cleverness and wit on the part of the Western negotiator will be respected.

The same applies when setting up businesses or establishing subsidiaries. Government approval can be a long and slow and frustrating process. Searching for suitable staff takes time, longer than it might in the West, especially in countries where the education system is less advanced and/or the job market is tight. Prior research can alert the manager to some of these problems in advance and allow him or her to prepare, but a waiting game is still necessary. Westerners from northern climates should be aware too that heat and humidity will also act as a drain on physical and mental energy. Even simple tasks, even where one is not reliant on others, can take longer than expected.

Most of all, though, patience is another of the cardinal virtues of the East. Studies have shown that Chinese businesses tend to have longer planning horizons than their Western counterparts. This may in part be a product of their ownership structures; numbers of public companies are fairly small, and even when companies do go public the original owners tend to retain a controlling interest, so there is less pressure for dividends and immediate growth. But the Confucian way of thinking is more oriented towards the long term. Patience is a virtue, haste is something to be avoided. This does not mean that Chinese businesses do not move quickly when the situation requires it; as we noted in the previous chapter, they are famous for their agility and ability to move quickly when an opportunity presents itself. But equally, they are capable of waiting for the right moment, and are probably better at this than many of their more impatient Western counterparts.

5 *Respect the hierarchy*. As noted, South-East Asian peoples value age and seniority. Elders are treated with respect, even veneration. Age is equated with wisdom. When meeting older people, treat them with polite deference and do not attempt to take precedence over them.

The same is true of people in senior positions. One of the things that often happens on a first meeting is the careful establishment of rank and precedence. Your opposite numbers will want to know who you are and what position you occupy in your own firm; in other words, how senior (or junior) you are. The treatment you will receive will depend on a combination of your own seniority and that of your opposite numbers. It is always a good idea to try to find out in advance who will be attending a meeting. If senior people are attending, try to ensure that your own side sends senior people as well.

Westerners are sometimes thrown off by the fact that, when meeting with a team of Chinese negotiators, the man who does most of the talking and appears to be in charge may turn out not to be the real leader. There is a tradition of self-effacing leadership in South-East Asia, as there is in China. The real leader sits back and watches quietly while the subordinates take charge. This is not universal, but examples can be found. Lee Kwan Yew, the creator of modern Singapore and widely acknowledged leader of the republic, has for several decades held no post higher than vice-president. For the last several years of his life, Deng Xiaoping was the undisputed leader of China, but his only official post was as president of the national federation of bridge clubs. Chinese folklore is full of tales in which the elderly sweeper standing humbly to one side of the court suddenly turns out to be the real king or emperor. These are extreme examples, but do not be surprised if the quiet man who sits near the foot of the table, watching and saying nothing, turns out to be the real boss.

6 Accept that government always has a role to play. As remarked earlier in the book, in South-East Asia, politics and economics are closely intertwined. Governments of whatever persuasion take a close interest in the economy. Singapore, Malaysia, Indonesia, Vietnam and, intermittently, Thailand all have what might be called 'interventionist economies', and government can and does intervene not only in the economy at large but in the affairs of individual firms.

Direct meddling is not so common as it once was, as governments begin to see the value of letting businesses get on with things. Malaysia has relaxed some of its laws on the composition of management teams; it is no longer necessary to have at least one *bumiputra* manager for every foreign manager brought in, for example. But government presence, if less overt, is still there. It is still a good idea to cultivate links with the relevant government ministries in the countries where a Western firm desires to operate. Good relations with government will result in licenses and applications being processed more promptly, and in officials being more willing to share information. This is not a matter of corrupt practice, but simply of governments being more willing to do business with companies it regards as friendly.

Corruption does exist – it exists in most countries around the world, it just gets talked about more in some than in others – and is a problem particularly in less developed countries such as Burma. It is sometimes argued that how one responds to corrupt offers ought to be purely a matter of conscience, and that each businessman or woman should decide for themselves whether or not to pay a bribe in order to secure business. In the first place, a distinction needs to be made between two different kinds of 'corruption': payments which are made to ensure that a service that ought to be carried out anyway is carried out in a timely manner, and payments to ensure that people break or bend the law. The first, which goes under a variety of names ranging from 'tips' to 'consultancy fees', is omnipresent in some countries, and payment of such fees is sometimes a necessary cost of doing business. Nor does it necessarily mean illegal practice, although one should be careful in countries such as Singapore.

As far as paying others to break the law goes, however, a little reflection will show that a decision also has to be made on sound business principles. First, if relationships are meant to be built on trust, how far can you trust an official whom you know to be breaking the law? If it genuinely is the only way to get action, then perhaps a case can be made. But the second point to consider is that once a bribe of this sort is paid – a payment to enable the breaking of the law – there is no going back. The next time a similar service is required, another bribe will be demanded, probably a larger one. And finally, the company will become a potential target. Word will spread, and others will begin demanding bribes too. Some people believe that corruption is endemic in the business culture of South-East Asia, and there is no getting away from it. That is wide off the mark. Cultivating a reputation for honesty and integrity can also be a powerful advantage.

7 Prepare for the changes to come. The story of South-East Asia is not over. Despite growth having been resumed after the Asian crisis of 1997, there is still much latent instability. In economic terms, the rise of China is posing a strong challenge for the entire region. Any Western business that intends to operate in South-East Asia must be prepared for change. We will discuss these changes in the following chapter, but meanwhile, Western firms and managers might to do well to try to cultivate some of the same agility and flexibility that are the hallmarks of the Chinese family business. Being prepared for change before it comes is half the battle; forewarned is forearmed.

These seven principles will not guarantee success. But following them will, hopefully, help businesspeople understand and come to terms with the environment within which they are living and working. South-East Asia can be a very rewarding place to do business, not just financially but in personal terms too. The people of this region are, on the whole, kind, generous, tolerant and happy. Working with them can be a source of pleasure as well as profit.

11 The Future

Over the past centuries, South-East Asia has served as, variously, a supplier of luxury goods to the lands to the north and the west, a centre of production of raw materials and resources needed by industrialised countries, a low-cost manufacturing centre, and a supplier of capital and investment, most especially to mainland China. Through all the various phase of its development, South-East Asia's economy has had one common feature: it has been largely based on exports. Unlike China, the United States or Western Europe, the internal market alone has never been enough to fuel strong economic growth.

Now, South-East Asia is approaching a new turning point. Can these countries continue to survive by exporting? Or can they carve out a new economic role for themselves which features a greater emphasis on self-reliance and sustainability? What role might the Overseas Chinese play in these developments? It is, of course, impossible to predict the future with any degree of reliability; no one can tell what South-East Asia will look like in fifty years time, or thirty, or ten. What we will try to do instead is identify some important trends, and then offer views as to what options might exist.

As noted earlier in this book, the balance of economic power between South-East Asia and China has changed. The Asia crisis showed how China, no longer heavily reliant on South-East Asian capital, was in turn able to help shore up the region's tottering economies. That case is even more true now, ten years later. Direct investment in China from the United States and Western Europe has increased dramatically. Chinese companies are raising foreign capital by listing on the stock exchanges of New York, London and other European centres. Indeed, Chinese capital has begun to flow back out of China, and big Chinese businesses are buying up Western companies and Western brands. The sale of its personal computer division by IBM to Legend turned the Chinese company into the world's third largest personal computer maker and gave it a global presence. This is just one high-profile example; there are many others.

This is not to say that China no longer needs investment from South-East Asia, or no longer welcomes it. It is simply that, as noted, the balance of power has changed. The Chinese economy has grown to such an extent that it now has an impact outside the borders of the People's Republic. Manufacturing is another case in point. In the late 1990s, the Chinese demand for manufactured goods seemed insatiable. So-called 'white goods' – refrigerators, freezers, washing machines and the like – were a major import. Ten years later, the market is saturated; there are hundreds of manufacturers inside China, so many that they in turn are being forced to export in order to survive. And these Chinese-based companies generally have lower wages and lower costs, and can compete very favourably; so much so that the World Trade Organization has had to act to prevent Chinese exporters from dumping cut-price goods and flooding the market. The same problem has occurred in textile markets, another area where South-East Asian firms had once had a competitive advantage. The spreading problem is affecting many manufacturing sectors, especially household and consumer goods.

Thus the relationship between the Chinese of the People's Republic and their overseas cousins is changing, and changing rapidly. China is on course to become one of the world's major economic power centres. Perhaps by as early as 2030, the Chinese economy will overtake that of the United States in terms of size. But long before then, China's economic influence will have spread around the world. Indeed, it is already doing so. And further, the Chinese government is very well aware of the country's growing economic strength. Not unnaturally, Beijing will try to extract advantage from this strength. The impact of the rise of China's economy is already being felt in South-East Asia, where as we noted earlier, China is increasingly making its presence felt in the councils of ASEAN and other regional economic bodies. Despite scare stories in some parts of the media, there is no suggestion that China is seeking political domination of South-East Asia; politically, the Chinese government still has its hands full at home. But the economic relationship between China and its South-East Asian neighbours is increasingly being shaped by China.

What might China need from South-East Asia over the next several decades? Despite China's growing economic clout, her development has been uneven, and large areas of the centre and west of the country still require modernisation and development. The Overseas Chinese will continue to find investment opportunities in China for some time to come, though they are increasingly competing with Western capital – and domestic Chinese capital – for these opportunities. And despite the rapid growth of higher education and the thousands of young Chinese going abroad to study in universities and business schools, there is also a continuing need for talented and experienced business managers. China's universities may be producing graduates at an unprecedented rate – so much so that there are fears of job shortages and unemployment among graduates – but the quality of their education is not always as high as it might be, and most lack experience of work and life outside of China. The managerial skills and greater experience of the Huaqiao business community mean that there will be a steady traffic of people going to and fro between South-East Asia and China for some time to come.

This increasing flow of people has incidentally highlighted the curious relationship that many Overseas Chinese have with the mother country. The current generation includes many whose parents, grandparents or great-grandparents fled China during the turmoil of the 20th century. Many still have family living in China. In interviews, they often express a strong sense of Chinese identity, and a desire to go back to the mother country one day, if only to locate surviving relatives. Yet when they do go back, many have mixed feelings. They find it hard to adjust to being in China; there is enough cultural dissimilarity between China and their own countries that they do not feel at home there. This is true even of people from Chinese ethnic groups with a very strong identity, like the Hakka or the Hui. Some who go back to China do not remain there for long. Indonesia or Malaysia or the Philippines may be lands where they are regarded as foreigners, yet for many Huaqiao, these lands feel more like home than does the mother country. This phenomenon is well-attested by many surveys and studies and Westerners are advised to remember that for all the strong cultural affinity between Overseas Chinese and China, there is often a distance between them as well.

Another import which China is likely to require in increasing quantity from South-East Asia is food. It is generally agreed that China's population is starting to stabilise. Exact figures are hard to determine, but it seems likely that the population will level off at a little over 1.3 billion before beginning very gradually to decline. But that is still a colossal number of people to feed. Further, it must be remembered that while China is the third largest nation by land area in the world, the majority of that land area is not suited to agriculture. And the fertile plains of the east, and the valleys of the Yangtze and the Yellow Rivers, China's traditional breadbasket, are also the areas that have seen the greatest growth and industrialisation. Productive agricultural land has been lost to housing, factories, highways and power stations. At the same time, though, mechanisation is improving farming outputs, and the danger of a 'Malthusian crisis' would seem to be passing.

However, it is a near universal trend that as countries become more affluent, its citizens consume more food per capita, and also demand a wider and more interesting variety of foodstuffs. In particular, meat consumption tends to rise markedly. This will happen in China; indeed, it is probably already happening. Food imports into China will almost certainly rise over the coming several decades, and much of this food will come from the rich, intensively farmed lands of tropical South-East Asia. Food has already been a major export from Thailand for several decades; it will be remembered that Thailand's first multinational company, Charoen Pokphand, began as an agrobusiness, and a good part of that business consisted of exports to China.

The People's Republic of China has a fairly rich range of natural resources, and is discovering and exploiting more, but its growing economy still requires imports of raw materials. It is not inconceivable that South-East Asia could again become an important exporter of mineral ores or tropical hardwoods, for example, but this time to China instead of to the west. The most important natural resource in the region, however, is oil. Chinese companies are already taking stakes in oil exploration ventures throughout the region. Rumours of large oil deposits in the southern reaches of the South China Sea have already prompted a certain amount of diplomatic scuffling between China and its neighbours, particularly the Philippines, Indonesia, Malaysia and Vietnam, all of which are nearby (there is a similar dispute with Japan over oil deposits in the East China Sea). Chinese interests here are concerned not only with securing oil resources for China itself, but with finding oil deposits that can be tapped and exported elsewhere. As with many other industrial sectors, China has a desire to take a hand in the global oil game.

Finally, just as Japan did in the 1980s, China needs markets for its exports. The affluent middle classes of South-East Asia offer such a market, and if the region remains stable and prosperous, then that market will grow. Chinese manufacturers hope that South-East Asian consumers will feel greater cultural affinity for their products and brands and will buy them in preference to Western brands. Whether they will do so in sufficient numbers remains to be seen, and Western brands do still have quite significant cachet. What does seem certain is that South-East Asian manufacturers will increasingly feel the pressure of Chinese competition.

One way and another, it seems inevitable that the nations of South-East Asia will grow closer to China, and that China's economic dominance will increase in line with its growing global economic power. There are dangers here. If Chinese economic domination becomes too visible, the indigenous population might begin to feel threatened, particularly in countries like Indonesia where there is a history of friction between the communities. But more generally, the rise of China poses both a challenge and an opportunity to all the countries and peoples of South-East Asia. Can they use China's growth to their own advantage? Might China's development prove a spur to the wider development and growth of the region? Can South-East Asia effectively ride China's coat tails to greater peace and prosperity?

Any answers to these questions would seem to necessarily involve the Overseas Chinese community, whose importance as a link between China and South-East Asia must surely increase. Once again, it seems, the Huaqiao will be called upon to play their role as middlemen, as conduits for capital and trade and skills in whatever form these are required.

But the answers also depend on political events as well as economic ones, and there are plenty of clouds on South-East Asia's horizon. The divide between rich and poor nations, and the income and educational inequalities within some nations, are compounded by political instability, terrorism, the threat of pandemic and, more generally, economic systems which still lack structure and transparency and where planning tends to be haphazard. In order to prosper in the 21st century, South-East Asia needs to get its house in order.

The divide between the rich, or comparatively rich, nations of the region, and the poorer nations is quite staggering. In Singapore, per capita incomes are as high as anywhere in the developing world. In Malaysia, Thailand and parts of Indonesia, these have been rising also. These are countries where, in the cities at least, the signs of affluence are immediate and obvious. But Burma and Laos and Cambodia remain locked in poverty. History shows that when rich nations and poor ones exist side by side, there is a strong risk of conflict. Reform and recovery in these damaged and backwards countries must be a priority, and the better-off nations of South-East Asia will have to realise that they have a role to play here, not just in terms of investment, but also providing skills, expertise and markets. Organisations like ASEAN can help to smooth out disputes and ensure that diplomatic friction between nations is kept to a minimum. In South-East Asia, as pretty much everywhere, peace and prosperity go hand in hand.

Even more critical is the problem of income inequalities within nations. Every country in the region suffers from this to a degree. The problem is perhaps most visible and most acute in Indonesia and the Philippines, where there is a great deal of wealth concentrated in a few small areas: northern Luzon in the Philippines, Java and eastern Sumatra in Indonesia. Both countries have their high-tech industrial parks and gleaming office buildings, and both have tens of millions of people living well below the poverty line. In part this problem is one of geography; both nations are island groups, and there has been a tendency for wealth to be concentrated on the island where the capital city and main economic centre is located. But this concentration is not inevitable, and sound economic planning and policies to bring development to the outer regions could make an impact. Other countries suffer from the same problem. Northern and eastern Burma are, if possible, even more backward and undeveloped than the southern Irrawaddy delta. Apart from its beach resorts, southern Thailand, in the Isthmus of Kra and beyond, also lags behind Bangkok and the centre, and this is a causal factor in the simmering discontent to be found in the south. The interior highlands of Vietnam are lagging behind the coast. Of course, uneven economic development is a problem everywhere, and contemporary Britain and America have the economic 'black spots' and regions afflicted with poverty. But the divide is sharper and more obvious in South-East Asia, and because of this, when tensions do arise, violence is more likely to be the result.

Like many parts of the world, South-East Asia has been affected by terrorism. Although nearly half the world's Muslims live in the region, they are for the most part a peaceful people. The Moro independence movement in the Philippines, which has waged several violent campaigns against the government, is based in the Muslim population, but in the past the conflict here has been more a result of ethnic differences rather than religious ones. Sufism, the mystical branch of Islam which emphasises personal purity and knowledge through inner belief, has been the dominant force in Islam in South-East Asia since the faith first arrived there. The Wahhabi movement, the small radical group which believes that force is a legitimate means of extending Islamic influence and advocates the overthrow of non-Islamic governments, has had very little influence there. However, as the Bali nightclub bombing in 2003 and other incidents since have shown, it only takes a few determined radicals to create violence and mayhem. It is heartening that the Muslim-dominated governments of Indonesia and Malaysia are firmly opposed to the militant radicals and have cracked down hard on them. But there are also concerns that if the crackdown is too hard, a backlash could ensue. In Thailand, bungled military operations against a few disaffected Muslim insurgents in the south have brought a huge wave of support for the latter, among people who would not normally support an insurrection. The situation in southern Thailand is now becoming tense, and Muslim insurgents were blamed by the Thai army for a series of bombs in Bangkok late in 2006. Both sides find it convenient to invoke al-Qaeda and the Wahhabi movement more generally; the Thai army to show it is fighting against global terrorism, the dissidents to give themselves legitimacy and to appeal for outside help. In fact, as in the Philippines, the roots of the conflict are ethnic rather than sectarian.

The threat posed by H5N1, or bird flu, continues to hang over the region. The World Health Organization estimates the chance of a global influenza pandemic before 2011 at 100%. In other words, the WHO believes that it is not a question of whether such a pandemic will happen, but when. The pandemic may not necessarily be H5N1, although it is the most likely candidate. But all the great killer epidemic diseases of the past – typhus, cholera, bubonic plague – have spread from animals to humans in conditions where the two live in close proximity, and what is more, most have originated in South-East Asia, where the hot and humid climate provides ideal breeding grounds for viruses. So, if the WHO is to be believed, the next great global pandemic is now in preparation, and South-East Asia is a likely starting point. Certainly H5N1 is still alive and well there. Pharmaceuticals companies around the world are frantically trying to create antiviral drugs that will stop it, but experienced epidemiologists point out that antiviral drugs cannot be engineered overnight, and that H5N1 has so far shown itself able to evolve and mutate drug-resistant strains faster than the scientists can invent new drugs. The problem has been compounded by Indonesia's decision in 2006 to stop sharing medical information with the WHO; there are rumours of a partnership deal with a Western pharmaceutical company which wants exclusive rights to a new antiviral drug said to be in preparation. This is like playing with matches in a gunpowder factory.

If H5N1 does mutate into a strain that can be easily passed between humans, then the consequences could be catastrophic for South-East Asia. The disease itself is likely to make very many millions of people very ill, although current best guesses are that the death toll might be fairly low, nothing like that of the influenza epidemic of 1917–19 for example. But even the threat posed by the disease will be enough. In the first instance, quarantine measures will have to be enacted. The serious impact of these can be seen in microcosm in the recent SARS epidemic in southern China, which also briefly affected parts of Canada. Quarantine disrupted travel and trade to a very great extent, and had immediate and negative economic impacts in both countries. One of the biggest threats is to global supply chains. Modern practices of ordering goods 'just in time' rather than keeping large stockpiles on hand mean that the export goods on which South-East Asia still depends, car parts, other manufactured goods, textiles, must be able to be shipped as and when required. If quarantines close the ports and airports, then the factories will stand idle, and the people who remain healthy will be out of work. Investment will dry up, and the stock markets will fall, and the crisis will begin again. It would take only a few months of severe quarantine for many economies in South Asia to crash into ruin.

Despite the World Health Organization's pessimism, this outcome is not inevitable. Preventative measures, taken swiftly, might reduce or even eliminate the conditions in which the virus breeds. More urgently needed still are common mechanisms for control and isolation of outbreaks when they do occur, to keep the effects from spreading through the rest of the region – never mind the rest of the world. So far, there is little sign of such co-operation emerging. Again, pan-governmental bodies like ASEAN can play a role in, figuratively speaking, knocking governmental heads together and bringing about greater co-operation. One thing is certain; inaction on this issue is not an option.

Finally, the continuing immaturity of the financial and economic systems in many countries remains a source for concern. The reasons for this immaturity stem partly from a different business culture, as we noted in Chapter 9, and partly from inertia and lack of understanding, particularly on the part of regulators and policy makers. Honourable exception must be made for Singapore, whose financial markets are as transparent and carefully governed as those of the West. It is notable that the Barings Bank crisis, occasioned by 'rogue trader' Nick Leeson gambling away the bank's assets on the Singapore stock exchange in the late 1990s, had little effect on the exchange itself. This is because the exchange authorities moved swiftly and promptly to limit the damage and restore public confidence.

But Singapore's success as a financial centre has been due in part to the contrast between it and the countries around it. The lack of transparency and viable regulation in other countries is precisely what has made Singapore a safe haven. Contrast it with the bellwether state, Thailand. The Asian crisis of 1997–8 should be have been a wake-up call to the Thai authorities, and to some extent it was. Western consultants were employed to help effect a thoroughgoing reform of the banking system and its legal frameworks, for example. But then the reform effort stalled, as reform efforts in Thailand so often do. The late and not very widely lamented civilian government overthrown by the army in 2006 was said to be riddled by corruption. The Prime Minister seems to have spent more time plotting to buy an English football club than on governing the country. The new military government may be more honest but has little experience at running a modern economy, and foreign investors are increasingly jittery. This is a story which has now been repeated several times, not just in Thailand but in other countries in the region. The lesson, so emphatically demonstrated by Singapore, that peace and prosperity also require stability and an economic and fiscal system based on honesty and trust, does not seem yet to have sunk in.

Reform, then, is still needed if South-East Asia is to come to terms with its future. As we have remarked at several points, politics and economics are very closely bound together in South-East Asia, and economic and political reform need to go hand in hand. With this in mind, let us take a brief look at the each country and assess the likely prospects for each.

Two can be discounted almost at once. As long as the SLORC regime remains in power in Burma, no reform is possible. The military government there has set its face rigidly against reform of any kind, and Burma remains locked in a post-World War II timewarp that it looks like it will have to endure for many years to come. And Laos, poor and reliant still on agriculture, appears to have little to offer anyone from outside its own borders. Tourism is picking up, albeit in a very limited way, but will not be enough to rejuvenate the Laotian economy. Nor does it appear that the Vientiane government has either the expertise or the will to propel the country forward. The best hope for Laos is probably economic assistance from a larger neighbour, most likely Vietnam. Such assistance would probably mean Laos losing effective control of its own economy, but this might turn out to be a good thing, at least in the short run.

There may be light at the end of the tunnel for Cambodia. The discovery of significant oil reserves offshore in the Gulf of Thailand offers a productive resource to add to the growing tourist industry. Reliance on oil money is always a tricky thing, but if enough revenues can be ploughed back into economic development, it should be possible to not only alleviate the plight of the country's numerous poor, but begin to develop an infrastructure which might, in turn, attract more foreign investment. The problem that many observers see is whether Cambodia's government will be able to exploit this opportunity successfully. Cambodia's political system remains dominated by the memory of the Khmer Rouge years. Although the country is largely stable and peaceful, there is little appetite for political experimentation, and holding the status quo is a priority. It will take another generation, perhaps, before younger Cambodians free from these memories are able to take their country forward.

Vietnam's government remains communist, but Vietnamese communists from Ho Chi Minh onward have tended to be a pragmatic lot. Although Vietnam's communists were very much within the sphere of influence of Moscow, when the Soviet Union came to an end, Vietnam chose not to follow the rapid reform programmed enacted by Russia and many other post-Soviet states. Instead it looked to its neighbour to the north, and the *doi moi* policy has clear and obvious parallels with China's economic reforms. The flow of foreign investment resumed once the Asian crisis had passed, and Vietnam's growth, if unspectacular, has at least been fairly steady. It is now a popular place for Western companies to outsource production, particularly in relatively low-skilled sectors such as the textile industry, where its low wages means it can still compete favourably with China. Vietnam will not become an economic powerhouse, at least not any time soon, but it does offer an object lesson to other states on how stable government can help create the conditions for economic growth.

That lesson, as we have seen, has not yet been learned in Thailand. The present military government has announced that it intends to hand back power to a civilian government once elections can be called. This is good news, but there is no guarantee that the elected civilian government will be able to create stability either. Thailand, on paper, has many advantages; a large population, rich natural resources, a flourishing tourist industry, high levels of skills and education in at least Bangkok and the surrounding areas, and critically, very good relations between the Thai and Chinese communities, who as noted, are often hard to separate. But continuing instability, and especially a rise in the level of Muslim insurgency, and these advantages could come to nought. Reform and stability are essential if Thailand is to prosper.

Malaysia, after Singapore, is probably the most efficient and effective state in the region. The long-lasting government of prime minister, Mahathir bin Muhammad, had many characteristics, some good and some bad. Among the good, however, were political stability, and an ability to link that stability with economic growth. His ministers showed they could look outside the country and also that they had considerable foresight. The Look East policy may have had its racist overtones, but in encouraging Japanese investment, the Malaysian government made the right move at the right time. The lessons of the Asian crisis were learned, and the Malaysian financial system today earns consistent praise from foreign regulators. Not all is rosy in the garden; foreign journalists write of nepotism and cronyism with government, contracts being handed to favourite suppliers and the like. It is difficult to tell how widespread such practices are. But in general, while the Malaysian system may be less than perfect, it is at least working.

Malaysia faces a problem of a different sort. To some extent, the country has become a victim of its own success. Economic prosperity has brought about rising prices, and rising wages too. Increasingly, the country's exporters are finding it hard to compete with China and India. It is notable that Malaysia has not benefitted from the outsourcing boom to anything like the same extent as, says, China, Vietnam or the Philippines. The challenge facing Malaysia's economic planners now is to find a new basis on which to compete internationally.

Indonesia remains, as ever, difficult to pin down. The Indonesian economy has struggled back to its feet, and successive post-Suharto governments have brought stability, which in turn has encouraged foreign investment. Neither terrorism nor the tsunami appear to have done lasting damage to the economy. But the internal divisions that we spoke of earlier remain more sharply acute in Indonesia than any other country. Nor has Indonesia entirely resolved the role and influence of the Chinese population over its economy. If China does exert a growing influence over the region, and if this provokes new ethnic tensions between Chinese and other peoples in the region, then we may confidently expect this tension to come first and most strongly in Indonesia. And yet, Indonesia needs its Chinese entrepreneurs. If they depart, and take their capital with them, the Indonesian economy will collapse.

With its large population and diverse natural resources and already developed economy, Indonesia could, if things go well, become a major economic power in East Asia, a certain rival to Japan and able to at least hold its own against the growing power of China. But for this to happen, Indonesia needs a strong programme of internal political, financial and economic reform, and most of all, it needs to prepare the ground for a lasting peace between the Chinese and *pribumi* communities.

There has been slow progress in the Philippines following the shaky start after the end of the Marcos dictatorship. Again, the country has benefitted from a series of relatively stable governments, and although the Moro problem remains in the south, the country as a whole is peaceful. This has helped to bring in foreign investment, and the Philippines has been a prime beneficiary of the outsourcing movement. One legacy of American occupation was a good basic education system with English widely taught. With this advantage, following the Indian example, the Philippines began to market itself as a base for call centres, payment centres and a variety of other business services. Although nowhere near as successful in this regard as India, the Philippines have still done reasonably well. The main problem in the Philippines has been a kind of institutional inertia within government. Economic planning is basic, and there is need for some sort of programme to continue the country's development and take it forward.

That brings us to Singapore, which has not only seen the future but is moving towards it. Singapore's planners realised long before anyone else in the region that reliance on manufacturing was only a phase in the country's economic growth. Wages in Singapore are already too high for there to be much chance of attracting outsourcers in search of low wages and low costs. But in any case, the era of South-East Asia as a destination for low-cost manufacturing may already be on the wane. As we have noted, China can out-compete much of the region on cost. Even more important, new destinations have opened up in Latin America and Eastern Europe. Several European textile firms have recently switched their outsourcing production from Vietnam and Thailand to Turkey, on the grounds that the supply lines are shorter and it takes less time for finished goods to reach Western Europe.

Singapore's new vision of the future has two dimensions. First, of course, Singapore will remain the largest financial market in South-East Asia for the foreseeable future. Second, however, Singapore is now positioning itself as a centre for the creative arts and associated industries. Film-makers, fashion designers, designers and developers of Internet products are all being lured to Singapore by a combination of favourable tax regimes, a strong skills base and excellent infrastructure. In terms of film-making, there are already plans to challenge Hong Kong's domination of the East Asian cinema market. So successful has the city been at turning itself into an Asian centre of creativity and art that *Time* magazine was moved to describe Singapore as a 'funky town'. The description was meant partly in jest, but there is an element of truth to it. Singapore has shown how it is possible to re-invent an economy in order to adapt to changing circumstances.

And Singapore may also have shown a way for other countries in the region, at least, to those with the desire to reform and develop. Outsourcing will not last forever. Something new is needed, some new direction that will help South-East Asia keep pace with the rest of the world economy. For many centuries, the region has enjoyed prosperity thanks to its ability to export what the rest of the world needs: first luxury goods and medicines and dyes, then raw materials for the West's industrial revolution, then manufactured goods to the developing markets in China. Today, if we are as many commentators suggest in the midst of a 'knowledge revolution' where creative ideas are a key source of competitive advantage, then it follows that there is a high demand for knowledge and creative skills, and that these are becoming increasingly important commodities on the world market. And, thanks to strong indigenous cultures mingled with the influence of Chinese culture, along with very good education systems in part of the region, at least, there is no shortage of either of these things in South-East Asia. It may sound far-fetched, but in an era when Europe is already attempting to position itself as a 'knowledge economy' to compete with the industrial dominance of America, India and China, it should not be impossible for South-East Asia to do the same thing. And as we look to the future, it should not surprise us to see the Chinese entrepreneurs of the region, as they have been for so long, playing the role of middlemen, working with indigenous businessmen and businesswomen to develop the 'creative resources' of the region and export them to markets around the world. In other words, the product may change, but the game will remain the same.

Bibliography

Abegglen, J.C. (1994) *Sea Change: Pacific Asia as the New World Industrial Center*, New York: Free Press.

Adamson, S. (2000) 'Thailand's Party and the Hangover', *Corporate Finance Review*, January–February, pp. 3–11.

Allen, D. and Ngo, V.L. (eds) (1991) *Coming to Terms: Indochina, the United States and the War*, Boulder, CO: Westview.

Allen, G.C. and Donnithorne, A. (1954) *Western Enterprise in Far Eastern Economic Development*, London: George Allen & Unwin.

Ambler, T. and Witzel, M. (2000) *Doing Business in China*, London: Routledge.

Andaya, B.W. and Andaya, L.Y. (2001) *A History of Malaysia*, Basingstoke: Palgrave.

Athukorala, P.C. (1998) *Trade Policy Issues in Asian Development*, London: Routledge.

Athukorala, P.C. (2001) *Crisis and Recovery in Malaysia*, Cheltenham: Edward Elgar.

Backman, M. and Butler, C. (2002) *Big in Asia: 25 Strategies for Business Success*, Basingstoke: Palgrave Macmillan.

Baker, C.J. (2005) *A History of Thailand*, New York: Cambridge University Press.

Baker, H.D.R. (1979) *Chinese Family and Kinship*, London: Macmillan.

Balisacan, A. and Hill, H. (2003) *The Philippine Economy, Development, Policies and Challenges*, New York: Oxford University Press.

Barrows, D.P. (1905) *A History of the Philippines*, New York: American Book Company.

Bartlett, C.A. and Ghoshal, S. (1989) *Managing Across Borders: The Transnational Solution*, Boston: Hutchinson.

Bastin, J.S. (1994) *Sir Thomas Stamford Raffles*, Singapore: National Museum.

Baydoun, N., Nishimura, A. and Willett, R. (eds) (1997) *Accounting in the Asia-Pacific Region*, New York: Wiley.

Bayly, C. and Harper, T. (2004) *Forgotten Army*, London: Penguin.

Berger, M.T. and Borer, D.A. (1997) *The Rise of East Asia: Critical Visions of the Pacific Century*, London: Routledge.

Berry, J. and McGreal, S. (eds) (1999) *Cities in the Pacific Rim*, London: Routledge.

Bhattacharya, A.K. (2001) 'The Asian Financial Crisis and Malaysian Capital Controls', *Asia Pacific Business Review* 7 (3): 189–93.

Bond, M.H. (ed.)(1986) *The Psychology of the Chinese People*, Oxford: Oxford University Press.

Booth, A. and Ash, R. (eds) (1999) *The Economics of Asia, 1945–1988*, London: Routledge.

Bresnan, J. (1993) *Managing Indonesia: The Modern Political Economy*, New York: Columbia University Press.

Brown, P. and Lauder, H. (2001) 'The Future of Skill Formation in Singapore', *Asia Pacific Business Review* 7 (1): 113–38.

Brown, R.A. (1996) *Chinese Business Enterprise: Critical Perspectives on Business and Management*, London: Routledge, 4 vols.
Cady, J.F. (1960) *A History of Modern Burma*, Ithaca, NY: Cornell University Press.
Callis, H. (1942) *Foreign Capital in Southeast Asia*, New York: Institute of Pacific Relations.
Camoens, L. de (1940) *The Lusiad*, trans. R. Fanshawe, Cambridge, MA: Harvard University Press.
Chandler, D.P. (2000) *A History of Cambodia*, Boulder, CO: Westview.
Chapman, E.S. (1949) *The Jungle is Neutral*, London: Mayflower.
Chen, M. (1995) *Asian Management Systems*, London: Routledge.
Chen, P.S.J. (1983) *Singapore Development Policies and Trends*, Singapore: Oxford University Press.
Chew, C., Leong, C.H., Sugiyama, K. and Leong, S. (1993) *Human Resource Development in Malaysia: Japan's Contribution Since 1980*, Kuala Lumpur: Institute of Strategic and International Studies.
Chew, S.B. (1988) *Small Firms in Singapore*, Singapore: Oxford University Press.
Corpuz, O.D. (1997) *An Economic History of the Philippines*, Quezon City: University of the Philippines Press.
Day, C. (1904) *The Policy and Administration of the Dutch in Java*, New York: Macmillan.
Day, C. (1966) *The Dutch in Java*, Kuala Lumpur: Oxford University Press.
Dent, C.M. (2002) *The Foreign Economic Policies of Singapore, South Korea and Taiwan*, Cheltenham: Edward Elgar.
Dixon, C. (1991) *South East Asia in the World Economy*, Cambridge: Cambridge University Press.
Dixon, C. (1998) *The Thai Economy*, London: Routledge.
Drabble, J.H. (1968) *The Plantation Rubber Industry in Malaya*, London: University of London.
Drakeley, S. (2005) *The History of Indonesia*, London: Greenwood.
Drysdale, P. (ed.) (2001) *Achieving High Growth: Experience of Transitional Economies in East Asia*, Oxford: Oxford University Press.
Egerton, H.E. (1900) *Sir Stamford Raffles*, London: Fisher Unwin.
Elegant, R. (1991) *Pacific Century: Inside Asia Today*, London: Headline.
Faaland, J., Parkinson, I.R. and Saniman, R. (1991) *Growth and Ethnic Inequality: Malaysia's New Economic Policy*, New York: St. Martin's Press.
Fforde, A. and Paine, S. (1987) *The Limits of National Liberation: Problems of Economic Management in the Democratic Republic of Vietnam*, London: Croom Helm.
Fournereau, L. (1894) *Bangkok in 1892*, repr. White Lotus Press, 1998.
Freeman, N.J. and Bartels, F.L. (eds) (2004) *The Future of Foreign Investment in Southeast Asia*, London: RoutledgeCurzon.
Gardner, L.C. (1988) *Approaching Vietnam: From World War II Through Dienbienphu, 1941–1954*, New York: W.W. Norton.
Ghosh, M. (1968) *A History of Cambodia*, Calcutta: Calcutta Oriental Book Agency.
Giraud, A. (2003) *Transnational Corporations, Technology and Economic Development: Backward Linkages and Knowledge Transfer in South East Asia*, Cheltenham: Edward Elgar.
Godement, F. (1999) *The Downsizing of Asia*, London: Routledge.

Griffin, K. (ed.) (1998) *Economic Reform in Vietnam*, New York: St. Martin's Press.
Haley, G.T., Tan, C.T. and Haley, U.C.V. (1998) *New Asian Emperors: The Overseas Chinese, Their Strategies and Competitive Advantages*, Oxford: Butterworth-Heinemann.
Haley, U.C.V. (ed.) (1999) *Strategic Management in the Asia Pacific*, Oxford: Butterworth-Heinemann.
Hamzah-Sendut, A., Madsen, J. and Thong, G. (1990) *Managing in a Plural Society*, Singapore: Longman.
Heng, P.K. (1988) *Chinese Politics in Malaysia*, Oxford: Oxford University Press.
Herz, M.F. (1958) *A Short History of Cambodia, from the Days of Angkor to the Present*, London: Atlantic Books.
Hiebert, M. and Sitzer, J. (1996) *Chasing the Tigers: A Portrait of the New Vietnam*, Tokyo: Kodansha International.
Hill, H. (1988) *Foreign Investment and Industrialization in Indonesia*, Singapore: Oxford University Press.
Hobday, M. (1995) *Innovation in East Asia: The Challenge to Japan*, Cheltenham: Edward Elgar.
Hodgson, M.G.S. (1974) *The Venture of Islam: Conscience and History in a World Civilization*, Chicago: University of Chicago Press.
Hofstede, G. (1992) *Cultures and Organizations: Software of the Mind*, London: McGraw-Hill.
Hooker, V.M. (2003) *A Short History of Malaysia*, Chiangmai: Silkworm.
Hourani, A. (1991) *A History of the Arab Peoples*, London: Faber & Faber.
Hughes, J. (1967) *The End of Sukarno*, London: Angus & Robertson.
Hyma, A. (1942) *The Dutch in the Far East: A History of the Dutch Commercial and Colonial Empire*, Ann Arbor, MI: George Wahr.
Jackson, K.D. (1980) *Traditional Authority, Islam and Rebellion: A Study of Indonesian Political Behaviour*, Berkeley: University of California Press.
Jesudason, J.V. (1989) *Ethnicity and the Economy: the State, Chinese Business and Multinationals in Malaysia*, New York: Oxford University Press.
Jocano, F.L. (1988) *Towards Developing a Filipino Corporate Culture*, Quezon City: Punlad.
Jocano, F.L. (1990) *Management by Culture: Fine Tuning Management to Filipino Culture*, Quezon City: Punlad.
Jomo, K.S. (ed.) (2001) *Southeast Asia's Industrialization: Industrial Policy, Capabilities and Sustainability*, Basingstoke: Palgrave Macmillan.
Jomo, K.S., Fleker, G. and Rasiah, R. (eds) (1999) *Industrial Technology Development in Malaysia*, London: Routledge.
Jussawalla, M. and Taylor, R.D. (2003) *Information Technology Parks of the Asia Pacific: Lessons for the Regional Digital Divide*, Armonk, NY: M.E. Sharpe.
Kemasang, T.C. (1988) *The 1740 Chinese Massacres in Java: How Dutch Colonialism Created a Problem Minority in its Effort to Thwart Indonesia's Domestic Bourgeoisie*, Bradford: University of Bradford.
Khoo, B.T. (1995) *Paradoxes of Mahathirism: An Intellectual Biography of Mahathir Mohamad*, Kuala Lumpur: Oxford University Press.
Kolko, G. (1994) *Anatomy of a War: Vietnam, The United States and the Modern Historical Experience*, New York: Free Press, 2nd edn.
Komin, S. (1990) 'Culture and Work-Related Values in Thai Organizations', *International Journal of Psychology* 25: 681–704.

Krumm, K. and Kharas, H. (2004) *East Asia Integrates: A Trade Policy Agenda for Shared Growth*, Washington: World Bank.

Lasserre, P. and Schutte, H. (1999) *Strategies for Asia Pacific: Beyond the Crisis*, London: Macmillan.

Le Roy, J.A. (1914) *The Americans in the Philippines: A History of the Conquest and First Years of Occupation*, Boston: Houghton Mifflin.

Legewie, J. and Meyer-Ohle, H. (2000) *Corporate Strategies for Southeast Asia After the Crisis*, Basingstoke: Palgrave Macmillan.

Lim, L. and Pang, E.F. (1991) *Foreign Investment in Southeast Asia in the Twentieth Century*, Basingstoke: Macmillan.

Lloyd, G. and Smith, S. (2001) *Indonesia Today*, Singapore: ISEAS.

Lockard, C.A. (1994) 'The Unexplained Miracle: Reflections on Vietnamese National Identity and Survival', *Journal of African and Asian Studies* 29 (1–2): 8–17.

Mallet, V. (1999) *The Trouble with Tigers: The Rise and Fall of Southeast Asia*, London: HarperCollins.

Manich Jumsai, M.L. (1971) *History of Laos*, Bangkok: Chalermnit.

Manich Jumsai, M.L. (1979) *History of Burma: From Early Beginning to Modern Times*, Bangkok: Chalermnit.

Mann, R.I. (1994) *The Culture of Business in Indonesia*, Mississauga: Gateway Books.

McKendrick, D.G., Doner, R.F. and Hoggard, S. (2000) *From Silicon Valley to Singapore: Location and Competitive Advantage in the Hard Disk Drive Industry*, Stanford, CA: Stanford University Press.

McLeod, R.H. and Garnaut, R. (eds) (1999) *East Asia in Crisis: From Being a Miracle to Needing One*, London: Routledge.

Means, G.P. (1991) *Malaysian Politics: The Second Generation*, London: Oxford University Press.

Metraux, D.A. and Oo, K. (2004) *Burma's Modern Tragedy*, Lewiston: Edwin Mellen Press.

Milne, R.S. and Mauzy, D.K. (1980) *Politics and Government in Malaysia*, Vancouver: University of British Columbia Press.

Milton, G. (1999) *Nathaniel's Nutmeg*, London: Sceptre.

Morley, J.W. (ed.) *Driven by Growth: Political Change in the Asia-Pacific Region*, London: M.E. Sharpe.

Mortimer, R. (1974) *Indonesian Communism Under Sukarno: Ideology and Politics 1959–1965*, Ithaca, NY: Cornell University Press.

Mostrous, Y.G., Gue, E.H. and Martchev, I.D. (2006) *The Silk Road to Riches*, Upper Saddle River, NJ: FT-Prentice Hall.

Muller, G. (2006) *Colonial Cambodia's 'Bad Frenchmen'*, London: Routledge.

Murray, G. (1997) *Vietnam: Dawn of a New Market*, New York: St Martin's Press.

Murray, M.J. (1980) *The Development of Capitalism in Colonial Indochina (1870–1940)*, Berkeley: University of California Press.

Mutalib, H. (1990) *Islam and Ethnicity in Malay Politics*, Singapore: Oxford University Press.

Nguyen, C.N., Dinh, V.N. and Le, H.M. (1993) *Viet Nam: The Blazing Flame of Reforms*, Hanoi: Statistical Publishing House.

Nolan, P. (2001) *China and the Global Business Revolution*, Basingstoke: Palgrave Macmillan.

Ong, A. (1987) *Spirits of Resistance and Capitalist Discipline: Factory Women in Malaysia*, Albany: State University of New York Press.

Parkinson, C.N. (1937) *Trade in the Eastern Seas, 1793–1813*, Cambridge: Cambridge University Press.

Parkinson, C.N. (ed.) (1938) *The Trade Winds*, London: George Allen & Unwin.

Parry, J.H. (1963) *The Age of Reconnaissance*, London: Weidenfeld & Nicolson.

Pearson, H.F. (1956) *A History of Singapore*, London: University of London Press.

Phayre, A.P. (1883) *History of Burma*, repr. 2000, London: Routledge.

Pigeaud, T. (1976) *Islamic States in Java, 1500–1700*, The Hague: Martinus Nijhoff.

Pye, L. (1985) *Asian Power and Politics: The Cultural Dimensions of Authority*, Cambridge, MA: Harvard University Press.

Rae, I. and Witzel, M. (2004) *Singular and Different: Business in China, Past, Present and Future*, Basingstoke: Palgrave Macmillan.

Ramachandran, S. (1994) *Indian Plantation Labour in Malaysia*, Kuala Lumpur: Insan.

Redding, S.G. (1990) *The Spirit of Chinese Capitalism*, New York: Walter de Gruyter.

Richardson, S. (1991) *Southeast Asian Management: Cases and Concepts*, Singapore: Singapore University Press.

Richter, F.-J. (1999) *Business Networks in Asia: Promises, Doubts and Perspectives*, Westport, CT: Quorum.

Ricklefs, M.C. (1981) *A History of Modern Indonesia*, London: Macmillan.

Robequain, C. (1944) *The Economic Development of French Indo-China*, Oxford: Oxford University Press.

Robison, R. (1986) *Indonesia: The Rise of Capital*, Sydney: Allen & Unwin.

Robison, R. and Goodman, D.S.G. (eds) (1996) *The New Rich in Asia: Mobile Phones, McDonalds and Middle-Class Revolution*, London: Routledge.

Roff, W.R. (1967) *The Origins of Malay Nationalism*, New Haven: Yale University Press.

Roll, M. (2006) *Asian Brand Strategy: How Asia Builds Strong Brands*, Basingstoke: Palgrave Macmillan.

Rotter, A.J. (1987) *The Path to Vietnam: Origins of the American Commitment to Southeast Asia*, Ithaca, NY: Cornell University Press.

Runciman, S. (1966) *The White Rajah: A History of Sarawak from 1841 to 1946*, Cambridge: Cambridge University Press.

Ryan, N.J. (1976) *A History of Malaysia and Singapore*, London: Oxford University Press.

Sanceau, E. (1936) *Indies Adventure: The Amazing Career of Afonso de Albuquerque, Captain-General and Governor of India, 1509–1515*, London: Blackie & Sons.

Schlossstein, S. (1991) *Asia's New Little Dragons: The Dynamic Emergence of Indonesia, Thailand and Malaysia*, Chicago: Contemporary Books.

Shawcross, W. (1979) *Sideshow*, London: Andre Deutsch.

Shenkar, O. (2006) *The Chinese Century*, Upper Saddle River, NJ: Wharton School Publishing.

Shimizu, H. (1999) *Japan and Singapore in the World Economy*, London: Routledge.

Simms, P. and Simms, S. (1999) *The Kingdoms of Laos*, Richmond: Curzon.

Skinner, G.W. (1957) *Chinese Society in Thailand: An Analytical History*, Ithaca, NY: Cornell University Press.

Smith, R. (1968) *Vietnam and the West*, London: Heinemann.

Song, O.S. (1923) *One Hundred Years' History of the Chinese in Singapore*, repr. Oxford: Oxford University Press, 1984.

Stuart-Fox, M. (1997 *A History of Laos*, Cambridge: Cambridge University Press.

Sukma, R. (1999) *Indonesia and China: The Politics of a Troubled Relationship*, London: Routledge.

Tang, J. and Ward, A. (2002) *The Changing Face of Chinese Management*, London: Routledge.

Terry, E. (2000) *How Asia Got Rich: Japan, China and the Asian Miracle*, Armonk, NY: M.E. Sharpe.

Thompson, G. (1998) *Economic Dynamism in the Asia Pacific*, London: Routledge.

Thong, T.S.G. (1987) 'The Management of Chinese Small-Business Enterprises in Malaysia', *Asia Pacific Journal of Management* 4 (3): 178–86.

Torrington, D. and Tan, C.H. (1994) *Human Resource Management in Southeast Asia*, London: Prentice-Hall.

Tubanqui, H.R. (1982) *A Concise History of the Philippine*, Manila: Grolier International.

Tucker, S.C. (1999) *Vietnam*, London: UCL Press.

Turnbull, C.M. (1981) *A Short History of Malaysia, Singapore and Brunei*, Singapore: Graham Brash.

Van der Kraan, A. (1998) *Contest for the Java Cotton Trade, 1811–40: An Episode in Anglo-Dutch Rivalry*, Hull: University of Hull.

Vasil, R.K. (1980) *Ethnic Politics in Malaysia*, New Delhi: Radiant.

Vatikiotis, M. (1993) *Indonesia Under Suharto*, London: Routledge.

Villiers, T.F. and Earle, J. (eds) (1990) *Albuquerque, Caesar of the East*, Warminster: Aris & Philips.

Wade, R. (1990) *Governing the Market: Economic Theory and the Role of Government in East Asian Industrialization*, Princeton: Princeton University Press.

Warner, M. (1992) *How Chinese Managers Learn*, London: Macmillan.

Warner, M. (ed.) (2000) *Management in Asia Pacific*, London: Thomson Learning.

Warren, J.F. (1986) *Rickshaw Coolie: A People's History of Singapore (1880–1940)*, Oxford: Oxford University Press.

Watson, B. and Andaya, L.Y. (1982) *A History of Malaysia*, London: Macmillan.

Weidenbaum, M. (1996) *Bamboo Capitalism: How Expatriate Chinese Entrepreneurs are Creating a New Economic Superpower in Asia*, New York: Martin Kessler.

White, N.J. (2004) *British Business in Post-Colonial Malaysia*, London: Routledge Curzon.

Whitley, R. (1992) *Business Systems in East Asia: Firms, Markets and Societies*, London: Sage.

Williamson, P. and Wilson, K. (2003) *CP Group: From Seeds to Kitchen of the World*, Singapore: INSEAD Euro-Asia Centre.

Witzel, M. (2001) 'Coen, Jan Pieterszoon', in M. Witzel (ed.), *Biographical Dictionary of Management*, Bristol: Thoemmes Press.

Wong, S.L. (1985) 'The Chinese Family Firm: A Model', *British Journal of Sociology* 36 (1): 58–72.

World Bank (1993) *The East Asian Miracle*, New York: Oxford University Press.

World Bank (1998) *East Asia: The Road to Recovery*, New York: Oxford University Press.

Wyatt, D.K. (1984) *Thailand, A Short History*, New Haven: Yale University Press.

Yamazawa, I. (1998) *Economic Integration in the Asia Pacific Region*, London: Routledge.

Yen, C.H. (1986) *A Social History of the Chinese in Singapore, 1800–1911*, New York: Oxford University Press.

Yeung, H.W.-C. (1998) *Transnational Corporations and Business Networks: Hong Kong Firms in the ASEAN Region*, London: Routledge.

Yeung, H.W-C. (2002) *Entrepreneurship and the Internationalisation of Asian Firms*, Cheltenham: Edward Elgar.

Yoshihara, K. (1988) *The Rise of Ersatz Capitalism in Southeast Asia*, New York: Oxford University Press.

Young, G. (1988) *Beyond Lion Rock: The Story of Cathay Pacific Airways*, London: Hutchinson.

Yuan, G. (1991) *Lure the Tiger Out of the Mountain: The Thirty-Six Stratagems of Ancient China*, New York: Simon & Schuster.

Yusuf, S. (2003) *Innovative East Asia: The Future of Growth*, Washington, DC: World Bank.

Yusuf, S. and Evenett, S.J. (2002) *Can East Asia Compete? Innovation for Global Markets*, Washington, DC: World Bank.

Index

Guangdong 14, 15, 24, 38, 39, 58, 61, 62, 88

9781349543045